THE WAYS OF
GOD

THE WAYS OF
GOD

HOW GOD

REVEALS HIMSELF

BEFORE A

WATCHING WORLD

HENRY T. BLACKABY
& ROY T. EDGEMON

BROADMAN
&HOLMAN
PUBLISHERS

NASHVILLE, TENNESSEE

0–8054–2373–7

Published by Broadman & Holman Publishers,
Nashville, Tennessee

Dewey Decimal Classification: 231
Subject Heading: CHRISTIAN DEVOTION

Unless otherwise noted, Scripture quotations are from the Holy Bible, New International Version. Other translations are identified as follows: Moffatt: *The New Testament, a New Translation* by James Moffatt. Copyright © 1964 by James Moffatt. Used by permission of Harper & Row, Inc. and Hodder and Stoughton, Ltd. NKJV: New King James Version, copyright © 1979, 1980, 1982, Thomas Nelson, Inc., Publishers. Phillips: reprinted with permission of Macmillan Publishing Co., Inc. from J. B. Phillips: The New Testament in Modern English, revised edition, © J. B. Phillips 1958, 1960, 1972.

Library of Congress Cataloging-in-Publication Data

Blackaby, Henry T., 1935–
  The ways of God : how God reveals himself before a watching world / Henry Blackaby and Roy Edgemon.
    p. cm.
  ISBN 0–8054–2373–7 (hardcover)
  1. Providence of God. 2. God—Attributes. 3. Christian life. I. Edgemon, Roy T. II. Title.

BT135 .B55 2000
    231.7—dc21

                                                                00-031290

1 2 3 4 5 04 03 02 01 00

Contents

Preface

In 1989, Roy Edgemon crossed into the Communist side of Berlin through Checkpoint Charlie. Getting into East Berlin through the checkpoint was easy, once he showed his passport and bought East German currency. Stunned by the cruel contrast of his freedom as a tourist and the citizens' lack of it because they were residents, he was also overwhelmed by the poverty-stricken conditions on the Communist side of the infamous Berlin Wall. What could anyone do?

The wall was begun in 1961 to separate the free side of Berlin from East Germany. In the years following, many people had been caught or killed as they tried to get over or under the wall. Roy saw the rows of razor-sharp barbed wire and the machine guns that were trained on the wall—their purpose, to keep people on the Communist side from getting out.

Western governments had tried for years to have that horrible wall of death and separation torn down. Then, suddenly, the wall and its purpose began to crack. People on the East German side began to tear down the wall without being shot in the process. Television and newspaper reporters began to flood the world with the news that the Berlin Wall was coming down!

People on both sides of the wall began to demolish the hated barrier. Wars and threats of wars had not torn it down. The Cold War years of spying and intrigue had not brought it down. Diplomatic treaties and talks did not bring it down. As people by the thousands prayed, God brought down that wall in His sovereign time. There is no explanation for this historical event other than the hand of God. What diplomacy, even threats, could not do, God did!

Consider the Berlin Wall, fortified and guarded by an army, only to be torn down peacefully by civilians. Like the walls of ancient Jericho, the Berlin Wall seemed permanent. God revealed Himself in both places by eliminating both walls in unconventional ways. God's purpose in removing barriers we face is to reveal Himself to us and those around us. Revealing Himself to the world is one of God's ways.

As you read this book, I hope that the words of Scripture will be brought to life by the Holy Spirit, and that you will see that God's ways are not like our ways. But if God lives and works through us, the difference that only God can make will be apparent as His nature and ways transform us to become more like Him.

Henry T. Blackaby

Introduction

GOD'S WAYS ARE DIFFERENT from our ways! You can start in Genesis and go all the way through Revelation, and you will find that whenever God moves, it is not like anything you or I would have chosen to do. And yet, time and again, God chooses to work through His people to accomplish His purposes. If God's people desire to be on mission with Him to accomplish His purposes, they must understand His nature and His ways.

If you are in business, you have at least heard about seminars on business principles: about having a vision and setting your purposes, establishing your goal, setting your priorities. That is the way the world works, but it is not the way God works.

For instance, how might you or I have chosen to take the walled city of Jericho (Josh. 6:1–5)? Given the opportunity, we probably would have called in a military strategist, or read the latest book on the way other walled cities have been taken down. We might have consulted world rulers to see how they win victories. We might have even gone to work on a new kind of weapon.

How did God choose to bring down Jericho? In Joshua 6, God told Joshua, the leader of the Israelites, that Jericho was already in their hands. God had already given Jericho to them, and they would receive it in a way only God could have arranged.

God delivered Jericho to the Israelites in a way that would reveal Him to the land and the people. One way God revealed Himself was to have His people go in and take the land that He had given them. But they first had to believe that God had truly gone before them. Did God say something similar in Christ's command to "go and make disciples" in the Great Commission (Matt. 28:19–20)? Anytime God gives a command, He has already provided for its accomplishment. But we have to do the hands-on, "certain of what we do not see" (Heb. 11:1–2). Faith in Him is a way of God! God does not work apart from faith! So God's people followed His commands.

God's instructions for taking the land indicated another way of God. He used an approach that could only succeed through God's activity. God told Joshua to march the Israelite army around the city once each day for six days. The sacred Ark of the Covenant would be carried with them, led by priests blowing trumpets. On the seventh day this march would occur seven times, ending with one long blast on the trumpets followed by a loud shout from the Israelites. Then the walls of Jericho would collapse.

The Israelites could have used battering rams and long ladders to breach the walls. Man's experience and man's reasoning might have chosen man's way. They could have done that, but they would have missed God's purpose. God's purpose was not to take Jericho. God's primary purpose was to put the fear of Him in the hearts of all the kings in Canaan. This would allow His children to take the entire land. When God was through with that moment, the kings of Canaan did not fear the Israelites. They feared the God of the Israelites. They had no doubt that the God of the Israelites had brought down the walls of Jericho. That was God's purpose. He had purposed ahead of time to reveal Himself to the nations by the way He worked with His people.

God deliberately chooses not to use the ways of the world so that the world will know the difference that He makes. However, we are sometimes caught up in the ways of the world. We may try to baptize them into the kingdom and ask God to get glory from it. But God does not work that way. God's goal is first to reveal Himself to the world so they will know Him and be drawn to Him—not simply to accomplish a task. That is what this book is about. That is a way of God.

CHAPTER I

God's Ways Are Not Our Ways

"For my thoughts are not your thoughts,
  neither are your ways my ways,"
                  declares the LORD.
"As the heavens are higher than the earth,
  so are my ways higher than your ways
  and my thoughts than your thoughts."
                  —Isaiah 55:8–9

AS THE CREATOR AND RULER of the world, God's very nature is eternal and supreme. He is the Sovereign God. We are flesh and blood, created by God to serve God, placed in the context of time by God. It is no surprise that His ways are different from ours. What is surprising is how often we ignore or mistake that incredible difference. Not as surprising is that we overlook the main element of that difference—sin.

Sin is failing to walk in God's ways, or choosing not to follow them. Sin has affected everyone (Rom. 3:23); therefore, no human naturally has godly ways. We build our own cultures and societies, even within Christianity. We can easily make critical judgments and choices based on traditions, old or new, instead of looking to God's Word as the plumb line of eternal truth.

How can we recognize God's ways if they are not like our ways? The Bible provides instruction on how the Word of God can help us learn the ways of God. Some people have a tendency to select verses and use them out of the context from which they were written. Any verse they might choose will be true, but no one can understand the dimension of a verse without knowing what comes immediately before and after it.

God Makes Himself Available

Isaiah 55:6–11 is a tremendously helpful portion of Scripture. It says to seek God "while He may be found" because it is one of God's ways to make Himself available to us. Next, we encounter a little connecting word sprinkled throughout these verses. This word appears in most translations and supplies a context as we study. The connecting word is *for.* Whenever we see a connecting word in the Bible, it means that what we are going to read next is based on what came just before. We cannot understand what we are about to read unless we connect it to what we have read.

Isaiah 55:6 tells us that we cannot seek the Lord just any time we choose. You might say God is always available! Well, let the Scripture correct you. There were times when Israel sought the Lord, but God said that it was too late (Jer.11:14; Isa. 63:17) and He would not hear their prayers. Throughout the New Testament this statement also holds true. One example was when Jesus wept over the failure of Jerusalem to receive Him as the Messiah. "If you, even you, had only known on this day what would bring you peace—but now it is hidden from your eyes . . . because you did not recognize the time of God's coming to you" (Luke 19:42, 44). Do not

> Seek the LORD while he may be found;
>   call on him while he is near.
> Let the wicked forsake his way
>   and the evil man his thoughts.
> Let him turn to the LORD, and he will have mercy on
>   him,
>   and to our God, for he will freely pardon.
>
> "For my thoughts are not your thoughts,
>   neither are my ways your ways,"
>   declares the LORD.
> "As the heavens are higher than the earth,
>   so are my ways higher than your ways
>   and my thoughts than your thoughts.
> As the rain and the snow
>   come down from heaven,
> and do not return to it
>   without watering the earth
> and making it bud and flourish,
>   so that it yields seed for the sower and bread for the
>   eater,
> so is my word that goes out of my mouth."
>   —Isaiah 55:6–11a

presume upon God. His ways are not according to our way of thinking. It is crucial to know His ways and what the Scriptures say about them. It is our life!

Seeking God while He may be found also implies that there are times when it might not be possible to find God. Does it mean that God is not there? No, it means that there are some things that God says must be in place if He will hear us and respond.

What comes after *for* in these verses declares that God's thoughts are not our thoughts and His ways are not our ways. That is why we must call on Him and forsake wicked ways and thoughts so we can turn to the Lord and receive His mercy and pardon. God says in Isaiah 55:9:

> "As the heavens are higher than the earth,
> so are my ways higher than your ways
> and my thoughts than your thoughts."

But to understand the dimension of that statement we must see it in context of the inevitable results, the profound cause and effect of God's words and God's thoughts. Then the incredible truth becomes understandable.

God Forgives

Every expression of the ways of God in the Bible seems to go against the ways of men. Thinking as a human, Peter was ready to prevent the sacrifice of Jesus because a wise teacher and good friend might be lost in death. Peter was ready to deny Jesus the cross (Matt. 16:22–23). The cross was God's way. Peter's ways were not God's ways. The promised Messiah died sacrificially so that He would rise to live again and provide eternal life to all believers for centuries to come.

Isaiah said that when a wicked man turns to the Lord, the Lord will have mercy on him and freely pardon (Isa. 55:7). This Scripture reveals that mercy is another way of God. Mercy always humbles us. Grace does not. If we know what we really deserve and know that God removed the penalty from us at an awful cost, we may think without humility, *Thank you God that—no matter what I do—you are always there to help me.* God is there, but He will not bless us regardless of our sin. That is never God's way as is evidenced throughout Scripture. If we keep and hold sin in our heart, the Lord will not hear us (Ps. 66:18).

God's willingness to forgive us is certainly one of His ways. Forgiveness reflects the love of God. However, our focus in these days is too often on the grace of God when it needs to be on the mercy of God. Grace follows mercy, and mercy follows repentance. Confessing our sins is agreement with God. Repenting, or turning from the confessed sin, brings God's mercy. Repentance also means that we believe God will respond by withholding judgment and extending His own righteousness to cover our sins. God in His mercy is willing to forgive us and remove the penalty that we deserve. God's grace gives us what we do not deserve— exemption from the judgment. God forgives us because it is His way.

The apostle Paul is one of the greatest examples of God's grace and love that is found in the Bible. Paul lived the first part of his life as Saul. He was later called Paul.

Saul's theology was totally wrong. He was violently preju-
diced against Jesus and bitterly opposed to the Christian
movement. Saul persecuted Christians with blind zeal. He
agreed to the stoning of Stephen and voiced threats against
the church.

On the Damascus Road he was confronted by Jesus,
who said, "Saul, Saul, why do you persecute me? It is hard
for you to kick against the goads." Then Saul asked, "Who
are you, Lord?" "I am Jesus whom you are persecuting"
(Acts 26:14–15). Saul lived a religious life but did not have
peace with God. He would later say, "By the works of the
law shall no flesh be justified" (Gal. 2:16 KJV). Jesus
quickly answered that hunger in his life. Saul repented and
obeyed Jesus.

Can you imagine how Saul must have felt about his
actions toward Stephen and the others whom he had persecuted? He had to have been broken with remorse. But whatever guilt there was on Saul's conscience, Jesus washed it
away. Jesus may never have audibly spoken the words to Saul,
but Saul knew that his debt was paid and he was pardoned.
The past was as if it had never been. Saul later became known
as Paul, a new name to go with his new heart.

Look at God's pardoning grace in Psalm 103:10–12:

> "he does not treat us as our sins deserve
>   or repay us according to our iniquities.
> For as high as the heavens are above the earth,
>   so great is his love for those who fear him;
> as far as the east is from the west,
>   so far has he removed our transgressions from us."

Jesus also shared how grace sets you free when He said, "I tell you the truth, everyone who sins is a slave to sin. Now a slave has no permanent place in the family, but a son belongs to it forever. So if the Son sets you free, you will be free indeed" (John 8:31–32, 34–36).

God promised that He will abundantly pardon those who turn from wickedness:

> "As the rain and the snow
>   come down from heaven
> and do not return to it
>   without watering the earth
> and making it bud and flourish,
>   so that it yields seed for the sower and bread for the
>   eater,
> so is my word that goes out from my mouth
>   It will not return to me empty,
> but will accomplish what I desire
>   and achieve the purpose for which I sent it."
>   —Isaiah 55:10–11

This is a crucial truth. When God speaks, it is so (Isa. 46:10). God speaks only when He intends to accomplish what He says (Isa. 46:11b; 14:24, 27). This is another one of the ways of God. When God speaks, He is already in the process of doing what He says.

God's Way of Faith

Faith is the confident expectation that God will do what He has said He will do. Faith is accepting God's statement as clear evidence of what we do not yet see (Heb. 11:1). However, faith is not blind. Faith is based on what we know about God. Living by faith will affect every part of our lives, from our families, to our workplaces, to our involvement in church. Faith is a way of God (Heb. 11:6). God chooses to work in and through a person who believes Him, trusts Him, and obeys Him.

Abraham is one of the greatest examples of faith. God made a covenant with Abram based on his faith in God (Gen. 12:1–3). Abraham was called Abram before God changed his name to reflect that he would father many nations. When God spoke to Abram, God said that He would be Abram's God if Abram would obey and trust Him. God would bless Him. Abram was seventy-five years old when he set out to follow God's direction to a new land and a new life (Gen. 12:5).

The faith of Abraham became the pattern of all faith that is acceptable to God, even to the point that God counted Abraham's faith as righteousness (Gen. 15:6). Even the good works of Abraham were nothing in God's sight; but Abraham's belief in God, expressed in his obedience, was credited as righteousness and was considered worthy by God (Rom. 4:1–3).

Romans 4:20–22 explains that Abraham was often confronted with ironies that seemed cruel. For instance, he was promised a son when, from a fertility standpoint, his body was "as good as dead" (Rom. 4:19). "Yet he did not waver through unbelief regarding the promise of God, but was strengthened in his faith and gave glory to God, being fully persuaded that God had power to do what he had promised.

This is why 'it was credited to him as righteousness'" (Rom. 4:20–22).

David also expressed this kind of faith in Psalm 25. He entrusted his soul to God, and declared,

> O my God, I trust in You . . . .
>
> Show me Your ways, O LORD;
> Teach me Your paths.
> Lead me in Your truth and teach me,
> For You are the God of my salvation;
> On You I wait all the day.
> —Psalm 25:2a, 4–5 NKJV

David's cry speaks for all who want to know God's ways. David stated a simple truth: the one who fears the Lord is the one whom God will teach His ways. The secret of the Lord is with those who fear Him, and it is they to whom He will show His covenant. Only those who fear and trust God's mighty power are offered the type of relationship possible through a covenant with God (Ps. 25:12–14). Trust in God is greater, higher, and more certain than the greatest trust humans can experience with one another; it is based on the nature of God.

God's Way of Holiness

Holiness is another way of God. His presence defines what is holy. Anywhere God puts His presence is sacred, set apart, holy, and completely dedicated to His use. As we go about our daily work, we find our workplaces to be very secular. Yet, if God is in us, the workplace is made sacred by His presence there. God's presence lives in each of His people, and anywhere God puts His presence is sacred (Ezek. 36:26–27).

When God met Moses at the burning bush, God told Moses to take off his shoes because the place where he was standing was holy ground (Exod. 3:4–6). Why was it holy ground? Because God was there. God's presence bestows God's holiness, and by His presence God also fills His people with His power to bless. We should be conscious of the presence of God every time we gather with other believers.

Where is God in our lives? Do we realize that our bodies are the temple of the Spirit of the living God? Do we realize that, wherever we are, God is there in us? And wherever God is is holy ground? There is no place we stand that is not holy ground. This is true, not because we are there but because God has chosen to be there in us. People encounter God every time they meet a Christian. Every time we encounter another believer, coming face-to-face with someone bearing the presence of God, we should be overwhelmed by God's presence. That is also why our lives are filled with the capacity to bless. It does not matter who we are with—God is there. God can choose to bless through the lives of those who are His own.

Holiness sets God's people apart. Isaiah said he saw "the Lord seated on a throne, high and exalted, and the train of his robe filled the temple. Above him were seraphs, each with six wings. With two wings they covered their faces, with two they covered their feet, and with two they were flying. And they called to one another,

'Holy, holy, holy, is the LORD Almighty;
the whole earth is full of his glory.'"
—Isaiah 6:1–3

When the disciple John was caught up into heaven in Revelation 4, he saw the same scene and heard the same song of the holiness of God. Holiness carries with it the idea of separation, or being set apart from the ordinary. But it is much more than that. The Bible teaches us that God is holy in His being. "God has spoken in His holiness" (Ps. 60:6 NKJV). He is holy in His speaking.

Holiness is more than separation from sin. However, holiness is the moral excellence of God. I once heard about a copy of the Constitution of the United States written so that, when it was held at a distance, the pattern of the letters looked like a picture of George Washington. The optical illusion illustrates that in the meaning of the words we see the character of men. The Constitution of Life is God's Word, the Bible. It is a portrait of the character of God. God's character contains His moral law. It is summarized in the Ten Commandments.

If we could take the Ten Commandments and shade the letters so as to make them show the face of God, we would have, as nearly as it can be had, an image of the quality of holiness in His character. A holy life is not an ascetic or gloomy life but a life lived by divine truth. Living a holy life means living above the standards of the world while still in the world. We can only do this as we give our lives totally to Jesus. Paul said, "It is because of him that you are in Christ Jesus, who has become for us wisdom from God—that is, our righteousness, holiness and redemption" (1 Cor. 1:30).

God's Way of Truth

In the Bible, God is called the God of Truth (Isa. 65:16). Because God is by nature Truth, everything He says, everything He promises, and everything He does is true. If He is true, He can be trusted and depended upon. Truth is a way of God, and it leads to life.

> Your statutes are forever right;
> give me understanding that I may live.
> —Psalm 119:144

God's Word is the standard by which all other words and deeds are measured. The psalmist said:

> Oh, how I love Your law!
> It is my meditation all the day.
> You, through Your commandments, make me wiser
> than my enemies;
> For they are ever with me.
> —Psalm 119:97–98 NKJV

God's Word is truth, and it both convicts us with the contrast between sin and God's truth, and provides and guarantees abundant life for those who believe Him and follow Him.

On the other hand, whatever is not true is a lie. The result of following a lie is the opposite of what happens when we follow truth. Death is the result of following a lie. The crucial difference between accepting and applying truth as opposed to believing a lie is seen in the Bible in Genesis 3. There in the Garden we see the first picture of

> Now the serpent was more cunning than any beast of the field which the LORD God had made. And he said to the woman, "Has God indeed said, 'You shall not eat of every tree of the garden'?" And the woman said to the serpent, "We may eat the fruit of the trees of the garden; but of the fruit of the tree which is in the midst of the garden, God has said, 'You shall not eat it, nor shall you touch it, lest you die.'" Then the serpent said to the woman, "You will not surely die. For God knows that in the day you eat of it your eyes will be opened, and you will be like God, knowing good and evil."
>
> So when the woman saw that the tree was good for food, that it was pleasant to the eyes, and a tree desirable to make one wise, she took of its fruit and ate. She also gave to her husband with her, and he ate.
>
> —Genesis 3:1–6 NKJV

sin among God's people. God said one thing, and Satan, in the form of a serpent, said the opposite. Adam and Eve had to decide who was telling the truth. To believe God, and therefore to obey Him, meant life. To obey the serpent meant death.

Choosing Truth

Jesus said that those who believed in Him and held to His teachings would truly be disciples and would know the truth (John 8:31–32). He told them the results: the truth would set them free. Because God is by nature Truth, everything He says is true and can be depended upon. Once we know what God has said and believe Him, we experience total freedom to live freely in God's way.

In John 17:17–20, Jesus also said that the truth separates and sets apart; it sanctifies. Jesus said that He is truth (John 14:6). Therefore, when His disciples were obedient to Him and went out into the world, they went as those who had been set apart. Before a watching world, they displayed Truth that would set free all who believed.

Jesus presented the dilemma of choosing between what is true and what is convenient, popular, or inviting. In Matthew 7:13–14, Jesus said that the way that leads to death is broad and many travel it. He also said, narrow is the gate and difficult is the way that leads to life, and few find it. Truth is always narrow and specific—but it is God's way to life!

Most people in our world are taking the way that leads to destruction. They are searching for success in their lives, marriages, businesses, or with their children. They want life at its best! When they started out, they followed the way that everyone was taking. But what most people fail to consider is God's way to success. The choices people make often bring the smell of success but fail in the light of truth. Like Adam and Eve, every believer in God has to decide who is telling the truth: God or the world? If they ignore what God has said, they never experience life. They will have to rationalize their lack of faith in order to answer God when He asks them why they left the narrow way of truth.

God told Abram that He would give him a son. This was not wishful thinking. Once God said it, it was done.

How God was going to do it and how long He would take was completely up to Him. Even if it took five years, Abram was going to have a son. Yet in the middle of that five years, Abram decided that God might need some help. The result was Abram's fathering a son by a chosen servant, Hagar (Gen. 16:1–15). God's response was that the child born of unbelief would forever be a source of conflict (Gen. 16:12). Unbelief is significant. Do not treat lightly what God treats seriously. God alone is Truth. What God says is always true—with no exceptions.

Rationalizing Truth

Human beings have a great weakness for rationalizing truth. Adam and Eve listened to that kind of rationalizing when they disobeyed the commands of God and ate the forbidden fruit. Throughout history, people have continued to redefine the clear teaching of God. The New Testament tells us that the scribes and Pharisees, who were the writers and interpreters of the laws of God, had developed all kinds of interpretations that were misleading and confusing to people. Jesus condemned those leaders and compared them to blind people leading blind people (Matt. 15:14).

This is why I speak to them in parables:
"Though seeing, they do not see;
   though hearing, they do not hear or understand."
—Matthew 13:13

In Luke 11:33–53, Jesus listed several disasters that would befall the Pharisees for loading people down with rationalized laws that the Pharisees didn't even obey themselves. This was not true of Jesus' teachings. Everything Jesus said came directly from the Father (John 17:6). Jesus spoke in a way that people could understand and obey. When Jesus spoke to the people about the things of God, they listened. Those who believed Him experienced God just as Jesus said. "This is why I speak to them in parables:

'Though seeing, they do not see;

though hearing, they do not hear or understand'" (Matt. 13:13).

In His Sermon on the Mount (Matt. 5–7), Jesus taught about what God wanted people to do and be. The crowd's response was amazement at His teaching. Jesus taught with the authority of truth, and "not as their teachers of the law" (Matt. 7:28). Jesus was God telling Truth. That was His nature.

The religious leaders echoed what others taught; Jesus was the voice of God. Religious leaders quoted human authorities; Jesus was the authority. The leaders split hairs over definitions; Jesus gave clear and definitive directions. They suggested investigations; Jesus gave insights to Truth. The religious leaders proposed exceptions to God's laws; Jesus pronounced eternal principles that applied to everyone.

Jesus talked about the real issues of life. "What shall it profit a man, if he shall gain the whole world, and lose his own soul?" (Mark 8:36 KJV). When men ask what life is all about, or what should be our aim or goal, Jesus has already answered, "Do not worry about your life, what you will eat or drink; or about your body, what you will wear. Is not life more important than food, and the body more important than clothes? . . . But seek first his kingdom and his righteousness, and all these things will be given to you as well" (Matt. 6:25, 33). People wondered about eternal life. Jesus taught, "I am the resurrection, and the life: he that believeth in me, though he were dead, yet shall he live" (John 11:25 KJV). "In my Father's house are many rooms; if it were not so, I would have told you" (John 14:2). This is Jesus, the Son of God, "the way, and the truth, and the life," (John 14:6). Those who believe Him experience everything He says. Jesus is Truth.

God's Kingdom Ways: The Parables

God also has kingdom ways. The ways by which He rules all creation are totally different from the ways used by those who rule the world. Jesus spent three and a half years reorienting His disciples from the world's ways to kingdom ways. Jesus taught His disciples the kingdom ways of God through parables that described His kingdom.

The Parables of Yeast and Mustard Seed

In the world, men plot, fight, market, and establish kingdoms by gaining the strategic advantage. God's ways are different. "The kingdom of heaven is like yeast that a woman took and mixed into a large amount of flour until it worked all through the dough" (Matt. 13:33). The presence of Truth in the world has life in itself in that it spreads and leavens as completely and effectively as yeast. A small amount of yeast or leavening can transform a large lump of dough. Likewise, God said His rule in the world spreads from pure Truth until the whole earth is completely touched and changed. God sent us His Truth in the

> He told them another parable: "The kingdom of heaven is like a mustard seed, which a man took and planted in his field. Though it is the smallest of all your seeds, yet when it grows, it is the largest of garden plants and becomes a tree, so that the birds of the air come and perch in its branches."
> —Matthew 13:31–32

form of a baby. Through Him, God would transform the world. Jesus' earthly parents were not prominent in the world's eyes. Yet, in the city of Nazareth, God guided them to raise the One who is the Messiah—Redeemer and Ruler over all mankind. Leaven is a kingdom way of God.

The mustard seed is small, and yet, when it is planted and grows, it becomes the size of a small tree, large enough for birds to nest in (Matt. 13:31–32). Like leaven, what the world would discount as too small to matter can grow to be something quite significant. In God's hands, nothing is too small. In fact, when His glory is revealed, He often uses what would seem foolish to confound the world's wisdom.

The Parables of Seeds and Weeds

To help His disciples understand how God extends His rule on earth, Jesus told two parables of seed. The parable of the seed that fell among the weeds reveals a way of God that helps us understand how God deals with His believers and with evil in the world (Matt. 13:24–30). Like the landowner's instructions to his helpers about the weeds, God's way is to leave the wicked for a season, lest pulling them out also uproot the believers. But at harvest time the weeds are to be pulled and burned. God's people clearly understood this teaching—it was real to life!

A farmer went out to sow his seed. As he was scattering the seed, some fell along the path, and the birds came and ate it up. Some fell on rocky places, where it did not have much soil. It sprang up quickly, because the soil was shallow. But when the sun came up, the plants were scorched, and they withered because they had no root. Other seed fell among thorns, which grew up and choked the plants. Still other seed fell on good soil, where it produced a crop—a hundred, sixty or thirty times what was sown.

—Matthew 13:3b–8

In another parable (Matt. 13:3b–8), seed fell on the path, in rocky places, among thorns, and on good soil. All the seed was good, but just as with truth, seed does not grow everywhere it is spread. Even though sowers of Truth offer it to everyone, some do not understand it, and it is snatched away like the seed on the path that was eaten by birds (Matt. 13:19).

Sometimes people receive the Truth with joy, like the seed that readily sprouted in rocky ground. But for truth, as with seed, if no roots grow, the new growth soon withers when trouble or persecution comes (Matt. 13:20–21). When men, like the seed that fell among the thorns, are surrounded by worries and the deceit of wealth, the truth they receive is choked and bears no fruit (Matt. 13:22). However, the good soil that receives seed is like the heart of the man who hears the Truth and understands it. In that person's life, the Truth will produce a crop that can yield even one hundred times what was sown (Matt. 13:23), and the yield of the crop supplies the abundance of seed that will grow the next crop.

Jesus was helping the disciples understand the ways of God as He brought lives to Himself. The seed was the Word of God. The soil was the hearts of men. All would depend on the condition of men's hearts. This was a way of God— that he would not force anyone to believe. The condition of each person's heart would determine that.

Assignments

Our service in the kingdom is accompanied by assignments. Everywhere we go presents opportunities to serve God in that place. Moses was given the assignment to lead the children of Israel. God's assignment for Moses was to lead the people in such a way that they would see God's ways. Moses knew the ways of God, and that made a difference. Without knowing God's ways, Moses would have acted altogether differently given his assignment.

> [God] made known His ways to Moses,
> His acts to the children of Israel.
> —Psalm 103:7 NKJV

The children of Israel did not know the ways of God. So they rebelled against God and thought it was all right (Num. 16:3). Some leaders came to Moses in rebellion against his leadership. Moses' response was to enter into God's presence and intercede for them (Num. 16:22), for Moses knew God and His ways.

Moses knew that no one can rebel against the ways of God and get away with it. The children of Israel knew the activity of God, but they did not know the ways of God. Because Moses knew God's ways, he interceded for them when he saw rebellion in the camp. To know the ways of God meant life and not death.

In the local church the same responsibility applies to God's people serving together. Think of one person that God has entrusted to you to intercede for instead of criticize. Make that one a prayer priority today. Since you now know this way of God, act accordingly.

The Way of Death

Rebellion against God leads to death. The way of God leads to Life. If we know God and His ways, we can be channels of spiritual stability and life to those around us because God's presence is in us (Ezek. 36:27). If we are spiritual leaders in our homes, churches, or workplaces, our positions have been accompanied with insights into the ways of God. We will know God's ways bring life.

If we are allowing the Holy Spirit to minister through us, we must say gently and firmly that there is no middle ground. There is no partial obedience. Partial obedience is disobedience.

The ways and thoughts of God alone bring life. Psalm 56:13 states:

> For you have delivered me from death
> and my feet from stumbling,
> that I may walk before God
> in the light of life.

Psalm 119:144 says that God gives understanding that results in life. Psalm 116:8 says, "For you, O LORD, have delivered my soul from death." Jesus said in John 10:10, "I have come that they may have life, and have it to the full." God's way is the way of life.

To turn away from or ignore the ways of God brings death. God gave the children of Israel a choice: "This day I call heaven and earth as witnesses against you that I have set before you life and death, blessings and curses. Now choose life, so that you and your children may live and that you may love the LORD your God, listen to his voice, and hold fast to him" (Deut. 30:19–20a). God offers us the same choice. Choosing life will allow us to experience what God has purposed for us from the beginning.

> The way of the LORD is a refuge for the righteous,
> but it is the ruin of those who do evil.
> —Proverbs 10:29

Sin Leads to Sin

Cain, son of Adam and Eve, wanted to offer God the fruits of the soil he had farmed. What God desired was the offering of a sacrifice. The produce Cain brought may have been outstanding in quality. What God valued, however, was the obedient offering of an animal sacrifice by Cain's brother, Abel. God showed Abel His favor. Cain became very angry. His partial obedience was disobedience, and disobedience brought death.

Rather than repent, Cain targeted Abel's obedience as the cause of his own rejection. Cain's sin led to more sin, the murder of his brother. Disobedience is sin and leads to further sin instead of a godly life.

Human nature says that the end will justify the use of any means. This is a deadly pragmatism. For the ways of God are as crucial as the end result. Having rational minds, we tend to use them to create substitutes for the ways of God. We are also likely to rely on the familiar for our choices instead of obeying God. The children of Israel were faced with knowing how to serve God in the midst of their relationships with others as they journeyed to the Promised Land. God gave them this admonition:

> "You must not do as they do in Egypt, where you used
> to live, and you must not do as they do in the land of
> Canaan, where I am bringing you. Do not follow their
> practices. You must obey my laws and be careful to fol-
> low my decrees. I am the LORD your God. Keep my
> decrees and laws, for the man who obeys them will live
> by them. I am the LORD."
>
> —Leviticus 18:3–5

A spirit of practical human reasoning as a substitute for
obeying God overshadowed the world in ancient times.
Human nature still operates this way today. The idea that
the end justifies the means influences the church. The reasoning of the world would say that God would accept a substitute for what He has asked us to do. The ways of God do
not change to accomplish immediate "success." God's ways
measure only our obedience or disobedience in doing His
will. The ways of God do not accommodate substitutes.
Substitutes are the reasoning of the world.

God is not concerned with accomplishing tasks. God is
interested in revealing Himself. This requires us to be available. Some people, like Cain, insist that God must accept
what we offer Him. However, what God values most is our
obedience. King Saul found this out the hard way—and it
cost him his kingdom (1 Sam. 13:13–14; 15:22–23).

God is working all around us to turn people from their
rebellious ways to His ways. The apostle Peter said God "is
not willing that any should perish, but that all should come
to repentance" (2 Pet. 3:9 NKJV). In the Book of Job, a
young man named Elihu confirmed for Job that even when
we are away from God it does not mean that God is not

working in our lives. Elihu encountered Job as he was talking with three friends about why he was suffering. Elihu began by admitting that he was probably too young to speak to the older men (Job 32:6). Then Elihu shared what he recognized as a way of God: God's way of working to reach, redeem, and restore people who are discouraged and rebellious. God's way is not rebellion and death. God's way is hope and life.

Think About—Pray About

As God said through Jeremiah: "'For I know the plans I have for you,' declares the LORD, 'plans to prosper you and not to harm you, plans to give you hope and a future'" (Jer. 29:11 NIV). We need to know His ways and His thoughts so we can identify and respond to His working in our lives. Meditate on God's plans. Are you available for His use?

- Think of one way the character of God overshadows the outline of your character. Thank God for His holy presence in your life.

- Jesus is the teacher who never had to revise His view or correct what He said. No culture can outgrow Him. No science will discredit Him. No authority shall supercede Him. Jesus is Truth. How closely are you following the Truth? Truth is one of God's ways for your life!

- Moses knew that the rebellion of the people against God could mean instant death for them. God's people did not realize this. Moses knew the ways of God, and this determined what he did. He interceded!

- When God gives you insight into the weaknesses of others, the insight is given for intercession, not criticism. Jesus constantly intercedes for us before the Father. Has He sent you as a messenger of hope to bring the good news of God's salvation? Are you prepared to tell someone what is available to him or her according to the ways of God?

CHAPTER 2

The Ways of God Are Love

Know therefore that the LORD your God is God; he is the faithful God, keeping his covenant of love to a thousand generations of those who love him and keep his commands.

—Deuteronomy 7:9

GOD'S NATURE IS LOVE, SO THE ways of God are love. God can never function contrary to His own nature. Never in your life will God ever express His will toward you in any way other than as an expression of perfect love. He will bring discipline, judgment, and wrath on those who continue in sin and rebellion. However, His disciplines are always based in love. Hebrews 12:5–6 speaks to this: "And you have forgotten that word of encouragement that addresses you as sons:

'My son, do not make light of the Lord's discipline,
    and do not lose heart when he rebukes you,
because the Lord disciplines those he loves,
    and he punishes everyone he accepts as a son.'"

Because God's nature is love, I am always confident that however He expresses Himself to me is always best. Two verses

31

that describe God's love to us are: "God so loved the world that he gave his one and only Son" (John 3:16), and "This is how we know what love is: Jesus Christ laid down his life for us" (1 John 3:16). Jesus is the most perfect example of God's love.

God Is Love

"God is love" (1 John 4:16). God is love personified, and we can know God's love through the person of His Son, Jesus Christ. God demonstrates His love for us in many ways. He created us and the world we live in and blesses us over and over with the beauty of His universe. In Psalm 50:1–2, the psalmist says, "The mighty God, even the LORD, hath spoken, and called the earth from the rising of the sun unto the going down thereof. Out of Zion, the perfection of beauty, God hath shined" (KJV).

Yet the most astonishing of any demonstration of God's love is the sacrifice of His Son for us. God created mankind in His moral image, and mankind broke His heart when sin marred the perfection of God's creation. Rather than let us face the penalty for our sin, the Father provided a remedy. But it required the death of His Son, Jesus Christ. It is God's nature to love! It is God's holy love that sent His Son to make it possible for marred mankind to be recreated in Christ. "Surely you heard of him and were taught in him in accordance with the truth that is in Jesus. You were taught, with regard to your former way of life, to put off your old self, which is being corrupted by its deceitful desires; to be made new in the attitude of your minds; and to put on the new self created to be like God in true righteousness and holiness" (Eph. 4:21–24).

In love God also provided for His Son's resurrection as well as His death (Eph. 4:9–10). All the hope in the world does not change the reality of suffering, but the love of God can change our response to it. The same love that caused Jesus to accept the cross for us is available to us even in adversity. The love of God is offered freely to us even at the ultimate cost to our heavenly Father and His Son. And in love He made His resurrection power available to us as well.

A story was once told about a bridgekeeper who spent his days working the massive gears on a pivoting railroad bridge that allowed boat traffic to pass on the river below. Each day he watched for the signals that told him to position the bridge parallel with the river for tall vessels to pass, or across the river for trains to travel over it.

One day a train approached the bridge without signaling the bridge keeper. With a start, he realized that the bridge was turned for boats and not connected to the tracks. The train would fall into the river if the bridge could not be pivoted back to touch both banks.

As the bridge keeper began to pull the lever to set the machinery in motion, he saw that his son was playing deep inside the gears. The train was speeding toward certain destruction, but to save the train and the unsuspecting people on it would mean allowing his son to be crushed. God knew the agony of such a situation.

> For God so loved the world that he gave his one and only Son, that whoever believes in him shall not perish but have eternal life.
>
> —John 3:16

God Has Chosen to Love Us

The Bible clearly shows that because of His nature God has chosen to love us. God loves everyone, even those who are unlovable to us. I once heard the story of a girl who left home to find work in a large city. Later her mother received word that the girl had become a prostitute. With a heavy heart the mother had a number of pictures made of herself and set out for the city. Not knowing where her daughter was, the woman went to every house of prostitution she could find. At each one she left a picture of herself. When the daughter entered one of the houses, she was astonished to see a picture of her mother. Written across the bottom of the picture was the words, "Come home. I love you." It was signed, "Mother." The girl left immediately for home. Every time we see a cross, the words written on it are, "Come home. I love you," signed, "God."

Romans 5:6–8 explains this truth of God's love and His making provision for us because of His love: "You see, at just the right time, when we were still powerless, Christ died for the ungodly." God revealed that His love does that. "Very rarely will anyone die for a righteous man, though for a good man someone might possibly dare to die. But God demonstrates his own love for us in this: While we were still sinners, Christ died for us."

God Teaches Us to Love

Our congregation in Canada had started a number of mission works. One that was forty miles away needed someone to move to that remote community and serve as a lay pastor. The congregation prayed, and a young couple responded. The husband was a college student, and the couple had little money.

If they moved to the mission community, he would have to commute to classes every day. I knew they could not afford to do this. I told them I couldn't let them. It would not be fair.

But the couple was deeply grateful that God had saved them. They knew what it had cost God to sacrifice His Son so that they could have a love relationship with God. The young man looked at me and said, "Pastor, don't deny me the opportunity to sacrifice for my Lord."

When this couple responded with such a deep sense of love and commitment, our congregation affirmed their sense of call. The same loving God who had saved them, in love, also provided for their needs.

God Does Not Want Us to Miss His Best

God's love wants perfection for us. His love wants to give every possible thing that is at His disposal. Perfect love withholds nothing, yet sin is real and denies us what love wants to give. So God is radical against sin—not against sinners, but against sin—because sin prevents us from receiving what perfect love brings.

Discipline is not the same thing as punishment. The purpose of discipline is training. God uses discipline to bring us back into a right relationship with Him so that we can receive His love. We can see the harshness of God in the Bible, but it is harshness against the sin that destroys humanity, the object of God's love.

God desires to preserve and protect the best He has for you and does not want you to miss, or lose, the best. That is the reason God demands obedience. He does not command that you obey just because He is to be obeyed. He requires obedience because He knows it is the only way that you can find and experience the abundant, eternal life He has provided for you.

Second Corinthians 9:8 tells us, "And God is able to make all grace abound to you, so that in all things at all times, having all that you need, you will abound in every good work." God's love has already appropriated the best on our behalf, having all that we need and "abounding in every good work." God's standard outlines His best for us and guides us to avoid sin.

God So Loved

God's heart cry to us is love. God's love continuously entreats humanity to open the door and be flooded with His abundant love. Everything God does is love, because He *is* love. Love is a person. God Himself is love! He would have to cease to be God not to love.

Because He is Love, God always takes the initiative in His love relationship. Because of sin in our lives, God must take the initiative (Rom. 3:10–18) and come to us if we are to experience Him. This is the witness of the entire Bible. God came to Adam and Eve in the garden. In love He fellowshipped with them, and they with Him. He came to Noah, Abraham, Moses, and the prophets. God took the initiative with each person in the Old Testament so they could experience Him in a personal fellowship of love.

This is true of the New Testament as well. Jesus came to the disciples and chose them to be with Him and experience His love. He also came to Paul on the Damascus Road. It is important for us in our relationship with God to remember that, in our natural human state, we do not seek God on our own initiative. But because God so loves us, He pursues a love relationship with us. Love, therefore, is a basic way of God in all His activity. His activity toward you will always be an expression of perfect love.

John 3:16 is one of the best-known verses of the New Testament. The message of this verse provides assurance of God's love for the world; God's purpose for us is that we believe in Jesus and not die; and God's promise of everlasting life. God loves us, and He has demonstrated His love over and over. God desires a love relationship with us.

The Assurance of God's Love

The Bible is a record of God's love. In love He created the universe, our world, and all that is within it. In love He provided salvation for Adam and Eve when they had sinned (Gen. 3:15). In love He gave Moses and the Israelites, whom He had already rescued, the Ten Commandments, so that all could know how to obey Him and live in a relationship of love with God, set apart for His use (Exod. 19:4–6).

> "As the Father loved Me, I also have loved you; abide in My love. If you keep My commandments, you will abide in My love, just as I have kept My Father's commandments and abide in His love. These things I have spoken to you, that My joy may remain in you, and that your joy may be full."
>
> —John 15:9–11 NKJV

It was also in love that God began to teach His people that He not only lived among them but what it meant to live in God's presence. From the moment He delivered them out of bondage from Egypt, He, in love, led them with His presence, in a pillar of cloud by day and a pillar of fire by night. God, in love, had made a covenant with His people, the Israelites.

The people were reminded of God's love with symbols of His covenant with them. The traveling temple, or tabernacle, that housed the Holy of Holies gave assurance of His presence. The law He had given them also reminded them that God wanted to keep them in a love relationship with Him. The feast days He assigned were also reminders of His love.

As part of the symbols of this covenant, God had His people to build an ark, or literally, container or altar, to be called the ark of the covenant. It represented the Holy Presence of God among His people, His desire to be among those He loved, and His requirement that they acknowledge His presence.

The ark of the covenant was constructed during the time of Moses (Exod. 25:10–22). God directed Moses to place objects in the ark that represented his presence and His promises. The ark was to be the container for the Ten Commandments, a golden jar of manna (the daily bread God provided like frost every morning for the Israelites in the wilderness), the staff of Aaron that had budded, and the covenants of God and His people. It was sometimes called

---

Whenever the ark set out, Moses said:
    "Rise up, O LORD!
        May your enemies be scattered;
        may your foes flee before you."

Whenever it came to rest, he said,

"Return, O LORD,
        to the countless thousands of Israel."
        —Numbers 10:35–36

the ark of Yahweh, or the ark of the Lord. In Numbers
10:35–36, there is a prayer song of Moses that would be
repeated whenever the Israelites set out as they followed
God through the wilderness. The ark always preceded the
people, because they depended on God to lead and protect
them. It reminded the people that the presence of God was
essential to their future and purpose.

Moses and the Israelites gained assurance of God's love
from the presence of the ark. But honoring God through this
sacred container was not God's ultimate purpose for His relationship with His people. Love is always an activity of the
ways of God. God expresses Himself very practically, reminding and teaching His people to love Him and obey Him. In
the relationship of love, He brings them assignments.

The Purpose of God's Love

God determined to love the Israelites (Deut. 7:6–9).
But do you realize that God likewise determined to love
you? Apart from His love, you never could become a
Christian, and God had something in mind when He called
you. So He began to work in your life, and you began to
experience a love relationship with God in which He took
the initiative. He began to open your understanding. He
drew you to Himself. All of this was done in love.

When you responded to His invitation, God brought
you into a love relationship with Himself. But you would
never know that love, be in the presence of that love, or be
aware of that love if God had not taken the initiative to love
you, personally. God's initiative in showing His love for you

was in motion thousands of years ago, even as He continued to work and reveal Himself to the Israelites (Isa. 32:6).

When the Israelites' wanderings in the wilderness ended, they settled in the Promised Land. Eventually God instructed them to build a temple that would replace the movable tabernacle they had carried with them throughout their journey. Like the temporary temple, the permanent one would contain a place that was most sacred of all, called the Holy of Holies. There, the ark would be housed, concealed behind thick draperies, and protected from the unworthiness of God's people and they from God's judgment. Yet God loved His people and made provision for maintaining His covenant with them. Only once a year, with meticulous preparation and elaborate ceremonies, could the high priest enter this sacred place to offer sacrifices on behalf of God's people (Exod. 30:10). This lasted until God provided a new covenant and an eternal high priest through the death and resurrection of His Son, Jesus Christ.

When Christ, as the Son of God, became the eternal high priest, He also provided us with access to the spiritual Holy of Holies (Heb. 10:19–23). The temple would no longer be an ornate structure made by human hands. The temple would now be one created by God—our own bodies (1 Cor. 3:16). Christ no longer entered this temple by means of the blood of goats and calves. He entered the most Holy place once and for all by His own blood, obtaining eternal, not yearly, redemption. The blood and ashes of animal sacrifices sanctified the priests so that they were outwardly sanctified or made ceremonially clean. But the blood of Christ cleanses us inwardly, purifying our hearts and washing our consciences from acts that lead to death, preparing us to serve the living God. The thrilling thing is that, in Jesus' atonement for us, we see not only His priestly duty exercised for us, but also we see His incomprehensible love, caring for us, providing for us, and showing us that this is God's purpose for us—to be loved by Him and live.

> When Christ came as high priest of the good things that are already here, he went through the greater and more perfect tabernacle that is not man-made, that is to say, not a part of this creation. He did not enter by means of the blood of goats and calves; but he entered the Most Holy Place once for all by his own blood, having obtained eternal redemption. The blood of goats and bulls and the ashes of a heifer sprinkled on those who are ceremonially unclean sanctify them so that they are outwardly clean. How much more, then, will the blood of Christ, who through the eternal Spirit offered himself unblemished to God, cleanse our consciences from acts that lead to death, so that we may serve the living God!
>
> —Hebrews 9:11–14

The Promise of God's Love

Jesus Christ, the Son of God, is mediator of a new covenant of love, "that those who are called may receive the promised eternal inheritance—now that he has died as a ransom to set them free from the sins committed under the first covenant" (Heb. 9:15). The first covenant brought both promise and penalty, while the new covenant brings promise and pardon. The result is eternal life.

No Substitute for Love

Some say that the English language is poor because it has only one word for love. However, the same language is rich in words that name substitutes for love. Any substitute is second best. When it comes to God's love, how could anyone substitute anything else in place of "how we know what love is: Jesus Christ laid down his life for us. And we ought to lay down our lives for our brothers" (1 John 3:16)?

Giving up your life so that someone else can live is as selfless as you can get. But giving up your life so that strangers can live—so that people who will ignore, curse, or deny your sacrifice can have the option of living—would be an extreme demonstration of unconditional love. That is the supreme example of God's love for us: sending His Son Jesus to us, and Jesus' loving us enough not only to give up His life for us but also to allow us to kill Him when it was for us He was dying (Rom. 5:6–11).

God gave us His law because He loved us. But our human nature would not allow us to become righteous under the law. Thus, we were condemned by the very law that was meant to save us. So God sent His Son, Jesus Christ, to be fully human and still fully divine, to live among us and die for us. Because of love, God allows us, condemned of our sins by the law, to be redeemed and found blameless, through the perfect sin offering, Jesus Christ. This is the message of salvation.

> Therefore, there is now no condemnation for those who are in Christ Jesus, because through Christ Jesus the law of the Spirit of life set me free from the law of sin and death. For what the law was powerless to do in that it was weakened by the sinful nature, God did by sending His own Son, in the likeness of man to be a sin offering. And so he condemned sin in sinful man, in order that the righteous requirements of the law might be fully met in us, who do not live according to the sinful nature but according to the Spirit.
> —Romans 8:1–4

Any Substitute Is Second Best

Sometimes in life we settle for less than the specific thing we want or need: a more practical car, a different color shirt, a smaller home. We can offer substitutes as well. When we offer substitutes for love to God or others, the results can be very serious. The difference with God is that His love is true, unconditional, and accessible to everyone, regardless of circumstances. Substitutes for love are contrary to God's nature.

During the Korean War, an American family received word that their son had been wounded, but that he would recover. He called his family often, first from a military hospital in Japan, and later from the American East coast. Then came the day that he called to say he was coming home. He told his family that he wanted to bring home a fellow soldier he had met in the hospital. They immediately agreed that it would be fine to have them both. The soldier said he was glad, because this buddy of his had thrown himself on a grenade to save the other men in a foxhole. "Bring him home, son. We want to meet this hero," they said.

"Well, he has to be in a wheelchair, because he lost his legs in the explosion. It would also mean a lot to me if you wouldn't mind letting him stay with us for a while."

They said, "If it means that much to you, we will try to fit him in."

The son went on. "He also lost an arm and an eye, and his face is not too pretty. "

"Maybe this is not a good idea, son. You come on home, but leave your friend in the hospital. The army is responsible for people who are injured that bad."

The young man protested, "He's my friend, and he doesn't have anyone else."

But his family said, "Come home alone, son. Your friend would never fit in here in his condition."

That night, they were notified that their son had taken his own life. When his body arrived for burial, they were shocked to see their son, his legs gone, an arm gone, an eye gone, and his face terribly disfigured. All he had wanted to know was how much they loved him and how he would be received.

You can offer God something you call love, when it is no more than a relationship on your own terms. And you can also settle for substitutes for God's love without even recognizing right away that you are. You can see everything as coming from God, and even begin to create substitutes for God's love that you aim for as if they were genuine. In churches believers have a thousand substitutes for God's love. It is all too easy to accept growing a big church, or being praised and admired as substitutes for God's love. Being known as "successful for God" can be a spiritually deadening substitute for God's love.

Rely on God's Love

As Jesus spent His last meal teaching and preparing His disciples, He assured them with these words: "Do not let your hearts be troubled. Trust in God; trust also in me" (John 14:1).

These lives that would soon come to understand the full love of God would be used to bring the same solution and comfort to others. The process would continue to this day. Those in whom Jesus Christ dwells live right next to the lives of others who are broken, hopeless, and helpless. That is because Jesus Christ, who is perfect love, flows out to others through the lives of those who know Him and know His love.

The "salt" of a Christian's life is the person of Jesus Christ. Christ makes our lives alive and real and full, with freedom to work through our lives in a broken world. All of our talents and abilities, all of our zeal combined, without Jesus, will not help our world one bit. For you see, the world has talents and abilities also. The world around us has zeal, but to our shame the world is often more zealous than Christians.

What then is the difference between Christians and the world? What makes a Christian salty? What causes believers' life to preserve and change those around them? The person of Jesus Christ, who is God's perfect love in us.

Paul said it clearly when he wrote that even with the tongues of men and angels, yet without love, the very person of Jesus Christ, you are nothing more than noise (1 Cor. 13:1). When people seek your advice, as a believer, you should offer Scripture as counsel, but be certain that you are offering it in love. God's love provided us with His Word, but others may not hear what you say unless God's love is flowing through you.

I once sat with a woman whose eyes immediately filled with tears as she told me about her sister, who just a month before had used a rifle to kill her husband. The husband had come home in a drunken rage and beaten his wife, the woman's sister. She could hardly lift herself from the floor after the beating. He staggered outside and encountered their grown son and began to beat him to death. The wife struggled to her feet, got the rifle he had left behind, and went to the door. She interrupted the beating by threatening her husband with the rifle. He came at her, and she pulled the trigger, killing him on the spot.

The woman telling the story wept with brokenness but was also grateful to Jesus Christ because she had once been like her sister, trapped in a lifestyle of destruction. Then she met Jesus Christ, and He had taken the idolatry, hatred, and immorality out of her life. Jesus' love had transformed her husband, too, and they were serving God together in their church, praising God and witnessing to His grace. The presence of the love of God can change the rotting flesh of lust to love. The decay of immorality becomes righteousness in the presence of God's love. Rely on God's love. He is trustworthy.

Function in Love

When God gives a command, it is to lead us into perfect love from Him. The purpose of the command is not for argument or discussion. Each command simply offers the opportunity to love Him more and to receive more love from Him. Paul stated, "Now to him who is able to do immeasurably more than all we ask or imagine, according to his power that is at work within us." Too often we think of Ephesians 3:20 as only a verse to encourage our faith. It is also a verse to encourage our obedience. We must do what God says for Him to manifest Himself through us.

> [God] is able to do exceedingly abundantly above all that we ask or think, according to the power that works in us.
> —Ephesians 3:20 NKJV

I remember a little group of eleven believers in Regina, Saskatchewan. Their mission church was struggling. The pressures and troubles of the community seemed too overwhelming and the response of the people was discouraging.

They had seen little growth and were so far past hoping that they had put a "for sale" sign up in front of their mission property.

I began to share with them, on a regular basis, something of the person of Jesus Christ. I said, "Let's sit with Him. Let's listen to Him. Let's watch Him. Let's see what He says that He is." Pretty soon that little group of people began to see that in Jesus Christ—if He is allowed the freedom to go out through lives—there is no telling what could happen through one solitary group of individuals who would dare to believe that the love of God can make a difference.

That little group of people began to believe that God had called them. They saw the infection of sin drawn out of people in the presence of Jesus. They saw families restored in the presence of the Lord Jesus. They saw that Jesus spoke the truth by saying that when He is lifted up He will draw all men to Himself.

Today, that little group has functioned for many years, starting at least eight missions, a campus ministry, a bus ministry, and a training center for young men. Wherever Jesus is fully and freely allowed to work through the lives of believers, He drives out the darkness and replaces death with life.

Making God's Love Known

Functioning in love is a way of letting the world know what God's love is. Jesus' purpose on earth was to make known God's love. John 17:25–26 says this: "Righteous

He replied, "You of little faith, why are you so afraid?" Then he got up and rebuked the winds and the waves, and it was completely calm.

—Matthew 8:26

When the sun was setting, the people brought to Jesus all who had various kinds of sickness, and laying his hands on each one, he healed them.

—Luke 4:40

The dead man sat up and began to talk, and Jesus gave him back to his mother.

—Luke 7:15

Father, though the world does not know you, I know you, and they know that you have sent me. I have made you known to them, and will continue to make you known in order that the love you have for me may be in them and that I myself may be in them."

Jesus was God expressing Himself as perfect love so that people would be drawn to Him. The leper, the woman at the well, blind Bartamaeus—all had personal experiences with the love of God as they received both hope and an invitation to a new life.

I once heard an illustration of love that placed the worth of another as first of all. A man had been invited to have dinner with a friend he had not seen in years. From the palatial home and the neighborhood it was in, the man could tell his friend had made a lot of money. In the equally elegant entry hall of the home, the man met his friend's wife and two young daughters. One of the girls had picked a bouquet of flowers. The other had gathered a handful of sticks, weeds, and scraps of paper. Later, when the man and his hosts went in to dinner, he was surprised—not by the china, crystal, and silver but by the centerpiece. It was an arrangement of the flowers one child had held and the sticks, weeds, and paper that the other had brought, too. His surprise must have shown on his face, because his hostess explained, "One of our daughters is a bit different from the other. All of us in the family work hard to show our special love for both of our children."

God Loves, So He Disciplines

Discipline means teaching, and disciples are those being taught. As a disciple, the discipline of God steers you to God's best and prepares you for ultimate judgment. Paul, in one of his letters to the Corinthians, captured this concept of being taught and being prepared. "So we make it our goal to please him, whether we are at home in the body or away from it. For we must all appear before the judgment seat of Christ, that each one may receive what is due him for the things done while in the body, whether good or bad" (2 Cor. 5:9–10).

There is no fear in love. But perfect love drives out fear, because fear has to do with punishment. The one who fears is not made perfect in love.

—1 John 4:18

Paul has an amazing intensity about this moment of judgment. He says that we make it our supreme goal, whether present or absent, to be pleasing to God. Then he says why. "For we must all appear before the judgment seat of Christ, that each one may receive what is due him for the things done while in the body, whether good or bad" (v. 10).

Now many of us would read the next verse and think something like this: *Therefore, knowing the love of Christ, therefore knowing the grace of God*, but that is not what Paul says. Paul says, "Since, then, we know what it is to fear the Lord, we try to persuade men." In the New King James Version, that verse is stated, "Knowing, therefore, the terror of the Lord, we persuade men." There is a clearer urgency in the second. But it is an urgency that comes from Paul's certainty that all will be judged. Paul's response is not anxiety over his own performance but compassion for those who are headed for the judgment seat of Christ without knowing Christ.

Love That Protects

It would be disturbing to know of someone who chose to pass up medicine that would save his life. After all, why would someone put himself in jeopardy when he knew there was a remedy? Paul knew what it means to fear the Lord. He also knew that all will have to appear before the judgment seat of Christ. For that reason, Paul said he persuaded people to accept the remedy for sin and condemnation—salvation through the Lord Jesus Christ and the honor of service to Him before judgment comes (2 Cor. 5:9–11).

When a vaccine for polio was discovered, the possibility of escaping a crippling, deadly disease seemed like a miracle. Millions had witnessed or experienced the pain and loss polio causes. Today we assume that because of the vaccine we are no longer threatened by the disease. However, few of us would recommend that our families and friends ignore getting vaccinated. In the same way, without the compelling knowledge of the love of Christ and the certainty of judgment, we can become tragically casual about the remedy for sin and suffer the consequences.

God Knows Us

Paul makes an amazing statement: "What we are is plain to God" (2 Cor. 5:11). Put another way, God knows us. When we come before Christ in judgment, the single most important factor is whether Christ knows us, followed by how well we have served Him. The question is not whether we know Christ. The question will be Christ's, when from His perspective He asks, "Have I had intimate fellowship with you? Have I been walking with you, knowing you, and calling you by name?" We will not be judged based on the qualifications we embraced, such as baptism or church membership. Paul knew this and said that it was his absolute passion to serve God. "Christ's love compels us, because we are convinced that one died for all, and therefore all died" (v. 14).

Keep My Commandments

The discipline of God shows His love as He presses in on us so we will not miss an ounce of what He has in store for us. John 15:9–10 says, "As the Father has loved me, so have I loved you. Now remain in my love. If you obey my commands, you will remain in my love, just as I have obeyed my Father's commands and remain in his love."

Obedience is a direct requirement for loving God and receiving His love. That is why God disciplines. If we understand more about God's love, it is easier to see why love compels Him to discipline us.

The New Testament was written in the popular language of its time, which was Greek. In Greek several words for love are each defined as different kinds of love. In English everyone uses the same word for love, whether talking about sports, work, home, food, or God.

Agapan is used in the New Testament 320 times. It meant something so deep that it was not often used in Greek literature.[1] Kenneth Wuest, in his book *Byways of the Greek New Testament,* defines *agapan* love, or *agape,* as "a love called out of a person's heart, an awakened sense

Be imitators of God, therefore, as dearly loved children and live a life of love, just at Christ loved us and gave himself up for us as a fragrant offering and sacrifice to God.

—Ephesians 5:1–2

of value in an object which causes one to prize it."[2] Wuest goes on to say that it is a love that recognizes the worthiness of the object loved. It is a love that comes from the recognition of the precious value of the object that is loved. It is a love of esteem.

Agapan love was exhibited at Calvary, when the heart of God was broken. God sacrificed His Son because of the preciousness of every lost person. God created mankind. He made us in His own image. He created us for relationship with Him. Even though we have been marred by sin, we are precious to Him, and He wants to see us remade into the image of His Son, into the very likeness of Christ. So God disciplines.

Think About—Pray About

To receive the benefit of the love God has already provided, every person must follow God's ways. Think about this: "He who did not spare his own Son, but gave him up for us all—how will he not also, along with him, graciously give us all things?" (Rom 8:32). Because of God's love for you, His will for you is always best. He is all-knowing, so His directions are always right. God is not only love, but He has also chosen to love you, deeply and profoundly. He provides you guidelines so you will not miss the full dimensions of the love relationship He offers you. Pray that you and those you influence will follow God's commands and receive all He has provided.

- With the new covenant of love comes the provision of eternal life. God's desire is to give us life more abundantly. God's ultimate promise is that we can live eternally and abundantly with Christ. Pray thanking God for His assurance of His love, His provision for your salvation, and His promise to you of eternal life.

- You rely on God's love in your life. Do you rely on His love enough to realize that others could rely on Him, too? Do you rely on God's love to remove your fear of the unknown or the anticipated? Do you rely on His promise to be trustworthy? Love, by nature, is trustworthy. Pray about your trust relationship with the love of your God.

- God points us to a door and, if we obey Him, God will manifest His love to us. Trust brings abundance, not necessarily in physical riches but in things that are eternal. Think about how God has manifested His love to you, and through you to others, as you have obeyed Him. Pray thanking God for those times when, because of God, you have functioned in love.

- The Father's commands bring life. They are not legalistic demands from an angry God. A command from the Father is an invitation from Perfect Love to see more of God's love than you have ever known. Directives come from God because He is ready to show you more of His love for you and reveal more of His purposes and ways (John 14:23). In this way, God's commands, like every word from God, are gifts to you from the One who loves you most. Think and pray about that.

1. Kenneth Wuest, *Byways of the Greek New Testament*, vol. 3 of Word Studies in the Greek New Testament for the English Reader (Grand Rapids: William B. Eerdmans, 1973), 112.
2. Ibid.

CHAPTER 3

The Ways of God Are Sovereign

"Praise be to the name of God for ever and ever;
  wisdom and power are his.
He changes times and seasons;
  he sets up kings and deposes them."
                                        —Daniel 2:20–21

WHEN I WAS A YOUNG BOY,
I had an experience that is still as fresh as though it happened this morning. I realized that God is God, and I am not. This moment changed my life to this very day! For every person who recognizes this profound truth, there are many more who do not. How will this truth affect a person's life? What does it reveal about God? Let's explore this truth.

What Does *Sovereign* Mean?

First, let me help you understand the word *sovereign.* Consider Daniel, from the Old Testament. He was a slave of the king of Babylon. He had been born free to a noble

Israelite family. But the king ordered a group of promising young men, a group Daniel was a part of, to be taken from their homes and brought to Babylon to serve in his palace (Dan. 1:3, 5). How could the king do this? He could do it because he was sovereign over his people and all those he conquered, such as the Israelites. Daniel came under the sovereignty of the king, who made him his slave, or servant.

Sovereignty can be a difficult concept for many in modern times. For centuries, rulers exercised sole authority and ownership over everything and everyone in their kingdoms. Nebuchadnezzar was the sovereign of Babylon. When he ordered Daniel and the other Israelite slaves to do things opposed to what would please God, some of them could have thought, *Well, God, you know that we want to honor you, but the king is telling us to do different.* Daniel and a few others knew that whatever Nebuchadnezzar thought he controlled, he was not above their Sovereign God. Daniel knew that God was Sovereign.

What, then, will it mean for us today to try to live under the conviction that the God we serve is Sovereign over all things, including our lives? The ways of God match the character of God! Since He is sovereign, His ways are absolute.

God Is Sovereign

To Daniel, did a king have greater power than God? Did he have greater control over things than God? Was Sovereign God not involved with the king of Babylon and his kingdom? Daniel's answer was confirmed by a change of circumstances. King Nebuchadnezzar of Babylon had a troubling dream. He summoned his magicians and wise men. To test them, he commanded that they tell him what he had dreamed, as well as what it meant. The penalty for failure would be death (Dan. 2:5–6).

As educated men, Daniel and his friends faced the same test: either they were wise enough to solve mysteries, or they were not. Daniel knew he did not know the king's dream, so he turned to Sovereign God who could tell him what no one else could know. Daniel urged his friends to ask God, not the king, for mercy and to deliver them with the truth (Dan. 2:18). God's response was to reveal the king's dream and the interpretation to Daniel in a vision. Daniel's response was,

> "Praise be to the name of God for ever and ever;
>   wisdom and power are his.
> He changes times and seasons;
>   he sets up kings and deposes them."
> —Daniel 2:20–21

This was Daniel's God!

Then the king ordered Ashpenaz, chief of his court officials, to bring in some of the Israelites from the royal family and the nobility. . . . The king assigned them a daily amount of food and wine from the king's table. They were to be trained for three years, and after that they were to enter the king's service.

—Daniel 1:3, 5

Earlier, when Daniel was younger, there had been another time when he had been faced with the choice of whom he would obey. He and his young peers from Judah were commanded to eat the king's best food. But it was food that had been offered to idols, as if the gods they represented were real. Knowing who God was, Daniel chose to obey God and disobey the earthly king. He and his friends drank water and ate plain vegetables, and God caused them to thrive (Dan. 1:15). The results were more than physical, and God also caused Daniel and his friends to excel above all the other learned men (Dan. 1:20).

Out of this background, Daniel called on God time and again for deliverance. My lifetime verse that has given me a background for serving God has come from Daniel 3:17: "The God we serve is able to save us . . . and He will."

God demonstrated Himself as sovereign and powerful through Daniel—and this was always before the watching eyes of the king. When Daniel revealed what God had shown him about the king's dream, the king made Daniel his special assistant. In addition, through Daniel, God also

Therefore we are always confident and know that as long as we are at home in the body we are away from the Lord. We live by faith, not by sight. We are confident, I say, and would prefer to be away from the body and at home with the Lord. So we make it our goal to please him, whether we are at home in the body or away from it.

—2 Corinthians 5:6–9

blessed the other young men. Along with Daniel, they remained faithful to God and were made administrators over the capital province (Dan. 2:49). Daniel's faith encouraged his friends to express absolute faith in their Sovereign God.

God Is in Control

Theologian and writer E. Y. Mullins said, "The holy and loving God has a right to be sovereign."[1] "When we say God is supreme we mean that there is no being above or beyond him, and that, in his nature and power, and in the qualities of his being, none other can be conceived of superior to Him."[2]

The sovereignty of God is another way of stating that God is in control. God's sovereignty influences everything in the universe. God is sovereign over His created order, and that includes every person and every power.

God's rule is ultimate and complete. All power that exists, exists because God allows it. He is sovereign over everything, including believers, and He intends for believers to acknowledge Him before a watching world through loving obedience.

When we hear of someone who dies in the prime of life, we might think the potential of that life was wasted. Payne Stewart, the pro-golfer, died tragically and young in a plane crash. Yet through his funeral, broadcast around the world, the gospel was presented to millions. Though Payne was in heaven with God, his witness was powerfully speaking as person after person described Payne Stewart's devotion and obedience to God.

Payne had recently given an interview in which he had remarked that all he wanted was either to live completely for God on earth, or go to live with Him in heaven. This is similar to what Paul said in 2 Corinthians 5:2, 5: "Meanwhile we groan, longing to be clothed with our heavenly dwelling. . . . Now it is God who has made us for this very purpose and has given us the Spirit as a deposit, guaranteeing what is to come."

Our Sovereign Instructs Us

When you honor God as your Sovereign, He honors you because His name is at stake. He marshals all the resources at His disposal to demonstrate that you are under a different set of rules. He can give wisdom beyond your capabilities and give you answers when no one else can find answers. He will provide the endurance needed to sustain your faithfulness.

The prophet Isaiah foreshadowed the experience of God's Son on the cross.

"The Sovereign LORD has given me an instructed tongue
    to know the word that sustains the weary.
He wakens me morning by morning,
    wakens my ear to listen like one being taught.
The Sovereign LORD has opened my ears
    and I have not been rebellious;
    I have not drawn back.
I offered my back to those who beat me,
    my cheeks to those who pulled out my beard;
I did not hide my face
    from mocking and spitting,

Because the Sovereign LORD helps me,
   I will not be disgraced.
Therefore have I set my face like flint,
   and I know I will not be put to shame."

—Isaiah 50:4–7

Isaiah realized that the test in chapter 50 was to trust God's sovereignty over life, even when others were trying to take life away. "Because the Sovereign Lord helps me, I will not be disgraced."

God Sustains Us

As God brought people into His path, Jesus was never taken off guard or unprepared. Because Jesus regularly prayed to the Father, He was always ready to respond to the needs of life with the very nature of God. Jesus only spoke what the Father told Him to say.

"Who among you fears the LORD
   and obeys the word of his servant?
Let him who walks in the dark,
   who has no light,
trust in the name of the LORD
   and rely on his God.
But now, all you who light fires
   and provide yourselves with flaming torches,
go, walk in the light of your fires
   and of the torches you have set ablaze.
This is what you shall receive from my hand;
   you will lie down in torment."

—Isaiah 50:10–11

Jesus was always ready for the needs of people because His heart was in tune with the Father's heart. The Son trusted and obeyed the Father. At the very beginning of His ministry, Jesus had spent several days teaching, preaching, healing, and also training His disciples. Yet the Scripture says that "very early in the morning, while it was still dark, Jesus got up, left the house and went off to a solitary place, where he prayed. Simon and his companions went to look for him, and when they found him, they exclaimed, 'Everyone is looking for you!'" (Mark 1:35–37). Jesus did not leave unannounced to cause them to worry or wonder where He had gone. He went out to pray. But the result of Jesus' necessary time alone with the Father was a renewal of His purpose, to preach truth to the people.

Jesus' healing of people in the region had caused a growing flood of the sick and demon-possessed to seek Him out. After he healed Simon's mother-in-law (Mark 1:31), word of Jesus' location spread quickly. The crowd of people desperate for healing came quickly. Jesus' response to Simon was, "Let us go somewhere else—to the nearby villages—so I can preach there also. That is why I have come" (Mark 1:38). As compassionate as Jesus was, the healing miracles served only as evidence of the Father's presence in Him and the Father's message He preached (John 14:11). Jesus obeyed the Father.

Sovereign over Creation

Earthly kings rule by inheritance or by seizing power from others. God, however, is Sovereign, not because of circumstances. God is Sovereign, because He is the Creator of all that is (Gen. 1:1). Psalm 33:6–7 describes God's power to create and His power over creation:

> By the word of the LORD were the heavens made,
>   their starry host by the breath of his mouth.
> He gathers the waters of the sea into jars;
>   he puts the deep into storehouses.

God does not rule because He took something from someone else. God is over all because He existed before anything else. He created the universe and everything in it for His purpose. He made humankind and cared for us (Ps. 8:4). He provided the remedy for sin that would otherwise separate us from Him (Eph. 1:4–8).

The words of Ephesians 1:4–8 declare that God intended for us to be here to serve Him. He chose us before He had even created the world.

> For he chose us in him before the creation of the world to be holy and blameless in his sight. In love he predestined us to be adopted as His sons through Jesus Christ, in accordance with his pleasure and will—to the praise of his glorious grace, which he has freely given us in the One he loves. In him we have redemption through his blood, the forgiveness of sins, in accordance with the riches of God's grace that he lavished on us with all wisdom and understanding.

"In love," He prepared to adopt us as one of His heirs. So that He could have a personal relationship with us, He committed to buying our forgiveness with the blood of His own Son. In advance, He provided undeserved favor, to be "lavished" on us with all of His wisdom and understanding.

God also rules over all other authorities and laws, solely possessing the power to forgive sins and provide life. "And having disarmed the powers and authorities, he made a public spectacle of them, triumphing over them by the cross" (Col. 2:15). Sovereignty is a way of God, the Creator.

Jesus demonstrated the power of God over creation when He showed that he was Sovereign over storms (Mark 4:35–41). He had only to command the storm to stop and it was done. Jesus also caused so many fish to come alongside Peter's boat that his nets began to break (Luke 5:1–6). God is Sovereign over creation.

God Can Do Anything

Every time I have gone through an earthquake, I have been reminded of the total sovereignty of God. When the walls begin to move and the light fixtures start swinging until they arch high enough to hit the ceiling, and the building creaks and the floor moves like waves under your feet—you suddenly realize that only the grace of God can stop the motion and save your life.

When the disciples were about to be swamped by the storm on the Sea of Galilee, Jesus spoke to the storm. He said, "Peace, be still." Jesus spoke with all the authority of the Creator to His creation. God can stop a storm or an earthquake because He is sovereign. He can save the vilest sinner because He is sovereign. He can raise up nations and take nations down. God does anything He wants to do because He is sovereign.

Sovereign over Worry

Nebuchadnezzar and the Babylonians are long gone, but God's sovereign presence remains and is active in the midst of His people today. However, things that can blind us to God's rule still surround us. Jesus declared the truth when He said, "No one can serve two masters. Either he will hate the one and love the other, or he will be devoted to the one and despise the other. You cannot serve both God and Money" (Matt. 6:24).

You might think, *Great! I know that money is not my master.* But are you making important life decisions based on the presence or absence of money? Do you determine whether or not to obey God depending on practicalities, such as "overhead"? If you do not immediately think of "no!" as your answer, you may be ruled by money more than you thought.

Even if you were quickly able to rule out money as a barrier to your service to God, there are plenty of other "practical" candidates for the job of master. Even after ruling out the potential of kings and money, that still leaves another frontrunner—worry.

Sovereignty is clearly a way of God. Yet worry can be a sign of doubt, evidence that we are not trusting God as sovereign over everything. How well do we witness to His nature as sovereign Lord and Creator if we continue to worry? Jesus taught about the dilemma some find in trying to serve the Father by offering this advice, "Therefore I tell you, do not worry about your life. . . . But seek first his kingdom and his righteousness, and all these things will be given to you as well" (Matt. 6:25, 33).

When believers worry, they actually may be trying to control a situation. They also may be revealing that they believe their situation is too difficult for God. But God has shown throughout Scripture that He has ultimate power over everything. He wants us to function under His lordship, trusting His sovereignty over this world.

God wants us to seek Him. The reward for seeking God, however, is His activity in and through our lives. When we serve our Sovereign, He will use us. Yet God never functions based on our will, but by His sovereign rule. God's purpose in working through you is not to help you to be successful or even worry-free, but to use your life as a means by which He reveals Himself. He is not there to reveal you to a watching world. He is there to reveal *Himself* to a yearning, hurting, and watching world.

Worry or Faithfulness?

Jesus had a great deal to say about worry when He preached the Sermon on the Mount (Matt. 6:19–34). Let's review: Jesus said that we first have to decide where we will store up our treasures—in heaven or on earth. He said all earthly treasures will either be stolen, wear out, or decay with age.

The night Roy and Anna Marie received their appointment to foreign missions, Baker James Cauthen, president of the mission board at that time, gave them their certificate of appointment and a charge. He said, "Roy and Anna Marie, take your treasures in your hearts and not in your hands as you go to Okinawa."

Several years later Roy asked Dr. Cauthen why he gave them that charge. Dr. Cauthen said he did not plan what to say. He just said what God put in his heart and wondered why Roy asked. Roy told him that in their first four years in Okinawa, they had been robbed several times, losing their typewriter, jewelry, and cameras, among other possessions.

Jesus said every believer would have to decide if God or things would rule their lives. No believer can serve two masters (Matt. 6:24). Jesus reminded us that we have a loving heavenly Father who takes care of all His creation, even the birds of the air. If God provides for them, surely He will provide for us.

A poem by an unknown author says,

> Said the robin to the sparrow,
> "Friends, I'd really like to know
> why these frantic human beings
>   rush about and worry so."
> Said the sparrow to the robin,
> "Friend, I think that it must be
>   that they have no Heavenly Father
>   such as cares for you and me."

I remember a story told about a great Bible teacher who stopped along the way on a cold and snowy winter day. He picked up a frozen sparrow that had died during the night.

He pulled his scarf from around his neck and wrapped it around the dead sparrow.

His students who were walking with him watched in silence as he walked to a toolshed, got out a pick and shovel, and dug a hole. He buried the sparrow, still wrapped in the scarf. He said, "I buried this little bird in honor of the One who was there when he died. Jesus said that God knows when even a sparrow falls." Someone has said that worry does not empty tomorrow of its sorrows—it only empties today of its strength.

Sovereign over Circumstance

God's purpose in working through you is not to help you to be successful but to use your life to reveal Himself. This is a crucial way of God. He is not there to reveal you to a watching world. He is there to reveal Himself to a watching world. One of the most common ways we cancel our witness to the greatness of God is by worrying and fretting. Often in situations, if we were to stop and meditate on His Word, we would have a deep sense of peace because we know God and we know that He is sovereign.

The difference between the daily lives of believers and those who are not Christians ought to be the believers' incredible sense of peace. God gives peace based on who He is and what He has made you to become as His child.

Whatever you do, whether in word or deed, do it all in the name of the Lord Jesus.

—Colossians 3:17

Knowing that God rules as sovereign in all of life reminds you that He is present in every circumstance. Where He is, peace ought to reign. People watching you go through the same situation that they go through should see the difference that your God-based outlook makes. They should be able to see the fruit of God's Spirit in you (Gal. 5:22–23).

Well-being

Some people have a nervous breakdown every time they look at the stock market because they base their idea of well-being, as well as their financial decisions, not on a relationship to God so much as on the trends in the market or on the last thing they read in a business journal. They frantically rearrange things to match what the world tries to tell them. Christians' responsibility is to be to the world the model of faith. They should be able to see someone functioning in the marketplace with the peace of the Sovereign God controlling his mind and heart. Or, even better, they may see God sovereignly providing for all our needs, including retirement, outside the stock market. Faith is based on the nature of God, the ways of God, and the provisions of God (2 Cor. 9:8–9).

J. H. Newman wrote a song that says:

> Lead, kindly Light, amid the encircling gloom;
>   Lead thou me on!
> The night is dark, and I am far from home;
>   Lead thou me on!
> Keep thou my feet: I do not ask to see
> The distant scene; one step enough for me.

"Do not store up for yourselves treasures on earth, where moth and rust destroy, and where thieves break in and steal. But store up for yourselves treasures in heaven, where moth and rust do not destroy, and where thieves do not break in and steal. For where your treasure is, there your heart will be also."

—Matthew 6:19–21

My dear friend was fighting a day-by-day battle with cancer. Yet God spoke great wisdom through his suffering. One day my friend said, "God told me not to let today be crucified between two thieves—yesterday and tomorrow."

Once when my friend with cancer was having a difficult day, I asked him if he had a word of wisdom from God. He said he had learned that day that God does not give dying grace on a nondying day. He did get that grace on the day when God was ready to take him home. He knew that God was sovereign over time and pain and even the moment when he would leave time behind.

Jesus promised in Luke 12:32: "Fear not, little flock; for it is your Father's good pleasure to give you the king-dom." Again, Jesus promised, "Peace I leave with you, my peace I give unto you: not as the world giveth give I unto you. Let not your heart be troubled, neither let it be afraid" (John 14:27 KJV).

Jesus said, "Don't worry at all then about tomorrow. Tomorrow can take care of itself! One day's trouble is enough for one day" (Matt. 6:34 Phillips). Jesus tells us that

we are to live in the presence, power, and love of God, day
by day. The psalmist said in Psalm 61:8, "Then will I ever
sing praise to your name and fulfill my vows day after day."

Sovereign over All We Have

Children have a way of watching our lives to see if we
believe what we say we believe. Since worry often seems to
be associated with finances, that is an even more important
reason for placing our confident trust in God. As a child, I
can remember many times our family getting right down to
the last of our money. But I also remember my father quoting a verse from the Psalms:

> I have been young, and now am old;
> Yet I have not seen the righteous forsaken,
> Nor his descendants begging bread.
> —Psalm 37:25 NKJV

Though we came down to our last cent, we never had to
beg. We watched God make provision. I have tried to live
that out in my life and family as best I know how, and God
has always provided, sometimes at the last minute. Now I
watch each of our children trusting God in their families for
God's daily provision.

God Provides

I remember a call from one of our sons, who was pas-
toring up in British Columbia. He asked me a sincere question. He prefaced it by saying, "Dad, we took a church of
seventeen, with all kinds of brokenness and difficulties. Now
it is growing, and in the last week we have seen a number of

O LORD God Almighty, who is like you?
    You are mighty, O LORD, and your faithfulness
        surrounds you.
You rule over the surging sea;
    when its waves mount up, you still them.
    . . . .
The heavens are yours, and yours also the earth;
    you founded the world and all that is in it.
                                —Psalm 89:8–9, 11

professions of faith. We are now seeing over one hundred attend. We have seen the gospel turn some lives completely upside down, and it's affecting adults, youth, and college students. We've never seen anything like it." Then he added, "But, Dad, why is it that when God is blessing so greatly, it is the lowest month for income? I don't know whether we are going to be able to get our paycheck from the church at the end of this month."

I could have immediately jumped in, but I waited. Then he said, "I know God is going to provide."

And then I silently said to God, "Father, I know you will, too. I don't know how you are going to do it, or how you can, but Father, would you make this a wonderful opportunity for our son and his little family, his whole church, and a watching world, to see that You can work exactly like this Scripture in his life?"

Shortly after, I was at a meeting in Georgia, and a pastor came to me and said, "Oh, Henry, I've got to tell you something. I was sitting in my office on Sunday, and a man just walked in, put a check on my desk, and simply said, 'I think there's a need in that little church in British Columbia.' He walked out. I looked at the check. It was for five thousand dollars." God did exactly what He said He would. God is Provider (Gen. 22:14).

The Infinite Capabilities of God

There is a sovereignty of God in the matter of trust and giving. In Mark 12:41–42 and Luke 21:1–4, Jesus did an unusual thing at the close of a very busy day. Mark says, "Jesus sat down opposite the place where the offerings were put and watched the crowd putting their money into the temple treasury. Many rich people threw in large amounts. But a poor widow came and put in two very small copper coins, worth only a fraction of a penny."

Notice that Jesus sat down and watched how people gave. There were thirteen collection boxes known as trumpets. Each of them represented one part of the ministry of the temple. They were called trumpets because the top of each was larger than the bottom. You could hear the coins as they clattered down to the box.

Many of the rich cast in much, but the poor widow put in two "thin ones," worth less than a penny. Yet Jesus said that the poor woman had given more than all the others (Mark 12:43). They gave out of their wealth and abundance, He explained. But out of her poverty, she had given all that she had. Her gift represented a great act of faith and the opposite of worry. She trusted in God to supply her needs and devoted all she possessed to Him.

It is comparatively easy to give out of abundance. But it requires strong faith to give out of poverty. The widow's gift was a great act of hope. Her heart was set on heaven and eternity. Jesus said, "Store up for yourselves treasures in heaven. . . . For where your treasure is, there your heart will be also" (Matt. 6:20–21).

"She of her want did cast in all that she had, even all her living" (Mark 12:44 KJV). Jesus had just answered a lawyer as to what was the greatest commandment. Jesus had answered, "'Love the Lord your God with all your heart and with all your soul and with all your mind and with all your strength.' The second is this: 'Love your neighbor as yourself.' There is no commandment greater than these" (Mark 12:30–31). This poor woman loved God and gave Him all she had. She loved her neighbors as well because the tithes and offerings collected in the trumpets were used for the needs of people and for worship. She was keeping the commandments of God by giving to Him and to her neighbors. Her giving represented faith, hope, and love.

Giving Recognizes God's Sovereignty

Paul said, in 1 Corinthians 13:13, "And now these three remain: faith, hope, and love. But the greatest of these is love." Giving a tenth of what we earn, called tithing, and all other kinds of giving, recognizes God's ownership over all we have. As we are faithful over the smallest amounts of money, God trusts us with His greater blessings in our lives. Paul also said, "Each man should give what he has decided in his heart to give, not reluctantly or under compulsion, for God loves a cheerful giver" (2 Cor. 9:7).

Jim Elliot, one of the five missionaries who died at the spears of the Auca Indians, wrote during his last year of college, "He is no fool who gives what he cannot keep to gain what he cannot lose."[3] Faith and trust in God is a choice. We can either worry or trust God who is Sovereign. We can insist on going our own way, or we can accept His wisdom and His guidance to know what to do.

Think About—Pray About

Jesus ministered in powerful ways, yet He looked to His Heavenly Father for His instructions and direction. "Don't you believe that I am in the Father, and that the Father is in me? The words I say to you are not just my own. Rather, it is the Father, living in me, who is doing his work. Believe me when I say that I am in the Father and the Father is in me; or at least believe on the evidence of the miracles themselves" (John 14:10–11). How well do you serve the Father? Can He rely on you to rely on Him for instructions and

---

The eyes of the LORD range throughout the earth to strengthen those whose hearts are fully committed to him.

—2 Chronicles 16:9

But the fruit of the Spirit is love, joy, peace, patience, kindness, goodness, faithfulness, gentleness and self-control. Against such things there is no law.

—Galatians 5:22–23

direction? Discuss this with your Heavenly Father, your Sovereign.

- Daniel did not choose to resist the system because of peer pressure. His choice was based on God's sovereign right to be Lord. Daniel's action revealed what he believed about God. Daniel knew that no man can serve two masters. Daniel believed the greatest danger was not the king's displeasure but God's. What God did in response manifested the difference God makes in a situation. Daniel made his choice and throughout his life remained obedient and faithful to God. Now would be a great time to pray to your Sovereign Lord and renew your choice to be obedient and faithful to Him.

- If what you are attempting is something everybody knows you could do, then others will see only you and not God. Often, when we make plans, we try to ensure success by being certain in advance that we know we can complete it. Then, God says, "Don't ask me to bless it, because it will not reveal Me. You know ahead of time that you can do it. It will simply let people know that you are a religious person." But when you walk by faith, with a confident trust in Him, based on what you know about God, His Word, and

---

And God is able to make all grace abound to you, so that in all things at all times, having all that you need, you will abound in every good work. As it is written:
"He has scattered abroad his gifts to the poor;
    his righteousness endures forever."
—2 Corinthians 9:8–9

His ways, then people can see God working. By seeing your God instead of you, they may come to know God.

- The Sermon on the Mount is, in its essence, our Lord teaching the disciples and helping them to get reoriented out of the kingdom of this world into the kingdom of God that functions in this world. Jesus never prayed, "Father, take them out of this world." He said, "I don't pray that you take them out of this world but that you keep them from the evil one" (John 17:15). God intends that we be light in the middle of darkness and salt in the middle of decay—revealing, preserving, and flavoring life by God's very presence. He wants us to be planted in the middle of our world but functioning totally different from the world. He wants us to live as those who know the Sovereign and do His will. Pray about it.

- You may not have all the resources you need. God purposed it this way so you would turn in faith to Him and come to know Him as your Provider. If, every time God creates the opportunity to display Himself, you worry and fret, take things into your own hands, or make your own decisions without reference to Him, you will never know what could have been. Remember, God is God, and you are not. Start trusting more deeply by allowing God to shape your prayer response to the truth that God is Sovereign over everything, even your possessions—and needs.

1. E. Y. Mullins, *The Christian Religion in Its Doctrinal Expression* (Nashville: Sunday School Board of the Southern Baptist Convention, 1932), 219.
2 Ibid.
3. Elisabeth Elliot, *Shadow of the Almighty: The Life and Testament of Jim Elliott* (New York: Harper & Brothers, 1958), 15.

CHAPTER 4

The Ways of God
Are Holy

And a highway will be there;
>   it will be called the Way of Holiness.
The unclean will not journey on it;
>   it will be for those who walk in that Way;
>   wicked fools will not go about on it.
>   —Isaiah 35:8

GOD IS HOLY! JOHN RECORDED that heaven proclaims, "Holy, holy, holy is the Lord God Almighty, who was, and is, and is to come" (Rev. 4:8b). Yet *holy* is a word that we may use without thinking about its meaning. *Holy* means "set apart, completely separate from and above all else." To us, God is the very definition of what holiness is; His way is perfect (Ps. 18:30). Believers are the chosen people of Holy God, set apart for Him (1 Pet. 2:9–10). We are His holy nation, a royal priesthood, serving and dedicated to the glory of sovereign God.

You are a chosen people, a royal priesthood, a holy nation, a people belonging to God, that you may declare the praises of him who called you out of darkness into his wonderful light. Once you were not a people, but now you are the people of God; once you had not received mercy, but now you have received mercy.

—1 Pet. 2:9–10

God's nature is different from ours; therefore, His ways are different from ours. His ways are always an expression of His nature. For instance, Isaiah says God's ways are like a highway over which He and His people travel. Because God is holy by nature, His way is a highway of holiness (Isa. 35:8). The same verse says that, because of this, "the unclean shall not pass over it." Any Christian desiring to experience God working mightily through him—whether leader or common person—but who has an unclean mind, heart, or life, *will not* experience God working through him (Ps. 24:3–6). One of the ways of God is holiness, and He will not work through an unclean life.

Through God's relationship with us, we are called to be like Him, to be holy as He is holy. The lives of believers are based on a relationship with the Father. That relationship can shape believers in such a way that their lives become a road over which God moves, bringing revival to His people and spiritual awakening to those who do not know Him. In order to do that, God requires the lives of believers to be a highway of holiness. God goes forth over and through holy lives. But what does it mean to be holy?

A Highway of Holiness

Holiness is God's requirement for relationship. Because of sin, our ways can even seem right in our own eyes, but the result of our ways will be destruction.

Because God is holy, we cannot stand in His presence without dealing with our sin. Psalm 24:4–6 explains that the one who can go up to His holy place is

> He who has clean hands and a pure heart,
>   who does not lift up his soul to an idol
>   or swear by what is false.
> He will receive blessing from the LORD
>   and vindication from God his Savior.
> Such is the generation of those who seek him,
>   who seek your face, O God of Jacob.

The one who can go up to His holy place has to meet God's standard of holiness. The result is that when he does he will receive both blessing and acquittal from God—his judge. This is the nature of every generation of those who seek the Lord. They will reflect and honor His holiness, as He Himself transforms their lives. He can also bless and vindicate the lost whom He will reach through His people, His highway of holiness.

Holiness in the New Testament

The concept of God's holiness shaping believers' lives is referenced again and again in the New Testament. Jesus said in His Sermon on the Mount,

> "Blessed are the pure in heart,
>   for they will see God."
> —Matthew 5:8

Peter said, "But just as he who called you is holy, so be holy in all you do; for it is written 'Be holy, for I am holy'" (1 Pet. 1:15–16).

Peter was quoting Leviticus 11:44–45, 19:2, and 20:7 as he repeated the Father's command that His people become like Him. This was one of those key times for God's people to be holy. God was marshaling them to be His highway across the Roman Empire. If they had not followed this way of God, they would not only have failed Him, but they would have also failed all those whom God wanted to use them to reach.

Sin in our lives is the antithesis of holiness and cancels our usefulness for God's purposes.

> But your iniquities have separated
> you from your God;
> your sins have hidden his face from you,
> so that he will not hear.
> —Isaiah 59:2

God's holiness is not mocked. He will not answer those who will not love and obey His standard of righteousness

A Warning

There was once a congregation where God was clearly at work. God's power was convicting and winning thousands of people to Christ. Many of the church members were selling land and houses and giving the money to their leaders to use for the many needy who were responding to the gospel. What better way to practice loving-kindness than to feed the hungry and house the homeless! How could believers do less in the face of devastating need?

One of the leaders in the church had just sold some land and brought the money to the church. A couple who were members were moved by the leaders' commitment and were inspired to do the same. The husband's family name meant "God has been gracious" and his wife's first name meant "beautiful." This couple announced that they were going to sell a piece of land and give the money for use in the kingdom of God.

The couple was known and probably respected in the church. They were not outsiders or enemies. They were impressed with what others were doing and genuinely wanted to do their part.

The land sold for much more than they thought it would, and evil entered their hearts. They decided to keep some of their windfall but say that they were giving it all, just as they had committed. They chose to lie and pretend that they had received no more than the expected price. Satan was trying to stop the work of God by using insiders to bring judgment upon the church.

But God gave one of the leaders boldness and discernment. When the husband came to present the money, he repeated his lie and fell dead. Shortly after, his wife came to see about him and was asked if the money given was indeed all they had received for the property. When she said yes, she fell dead also.

God is not mocked, especially His holiness! He desires truth and holiness from His people. This story happened two thousand years ago, and it appears in Acts 5:1–11.

As an old farmer once said, "God may not harvest in the fall, but He will reap His crop." The example of Ananias and Saphira may seem chillingly severe, but to those in the church, it underlined how serious and dangerous sin is, literally destroying lives and witnesses and undermining the cause of Christ. There is no escaping the harvest of our activities. When the heart departs, the actions depart, and the harvest follows. God can tell the condition of the heart by seeing the fruit of our living. "Do not be deceived: God cannot be mocked. A man reaps what he sows. The one who sows to please his sinful nature, from that nature will reap destruction; the one who sows to please the Spirit, from the Spirit will reap eternal life" (Gal. 6:7–8).

Abiding in Holiness

Holiness is a way of God. When holiness is present in God's people, there will be no hindrances to hearing His will, obeying His will, or God's accomplishing His will

> "Should you not fear me?" declares the LORD.
> "Should you not tremble in my presence?
> I made the sand a boundary for the sea,
> an everlasting barrier it cannot cross.
> The waves may roll, but they cannot prevail;
> they may roar, but they cannot cross it."
> —Jeremiah 5:22

through His People. Holiness in the lives of God's people is a sign of God's presence.

The abiding presence of God instructs and corrects believers through His Holy Spirit, who daily seeks to transform believers into the likeness of Jesus. When believers' lives bear the fruit of holiness, God is honored. Just as no plant, vine, or tree can bear fruit if it is not rooted and fed, believers can only grow in the holiness of God when they are rooted in Him. They must abide in the Father's holiness.

A common way to think about the word *abide,* as it is used in the Bible, is to think of it as describing living within the law. The word also means "to be rooted in, or to remain, or to continue being in a certain place, or to do things in a specific way." Jesus described what it means to live, or abide, in Him. He said His Father is the gardener, and He is the true vine (John 15:1). Believers are the branches of the true vine and are cared for by the gardener. Yet the kind of care the gardener provides in this illustration shows us the discipline of God. Jesus said, "He cuts off every branch in me that bears no fruit, while every branch that does bear fruit he prunes so that it will be even more fruitful" (John 15:2).

The Father disciplines us by pruning. He does this to remove the sin that prevents believers from being fruitful. The average Christian does not recognize the seriousness of sin. Just as the effects of pruning are apparent, believers know when God corrects them and know when God instructs them.

> "I am the true vine, and my Father is the gardener. He cuts off every branch in me that bears no fruit, while every branch that does bear fruit he prunes so that it will be even more fruitful. You are already clean because of the word I have spoken to you. Remain in me, and I will remain in you. No branch can bear fruit by itself; it must remain in the vine. Neither can you bear fruit unless you remain in me."
>
> —John 15:1–4

Accepting the discipline of God is something many would try to avoid. Yet correction by God leads to repentance and life—not only the believer's life but also the lives of those the believer impacts. Proverbs 16:20 says,

> Whoever gives heed to instruction prospers,
> and blessed is he who trusts in the LORD.

Accepting discipline from God leads to bearing fruit for God. Jesus said, "No branch can bear fruit by itself; it must remain in the vine. Neither can you bear fruit unless you remain in me" (John 15:4).

In the Old Testament, God's people were often pictured as His vineyard. However, they were not always pictured as a fruitful vineyard. Hosea described Israel as a luxuriant vine, but without fruit (Hos. 10:1). Isaiah compared God's investment in Israel with a farmer who invests in a vineyard only to find that the fruit it produces is wild and bitter (Isa. 5:1–7). Jeremiah brought the people this prophecy from God:

"I had planted you like a choice vine
of sound and reliable stock.
How then did you turn against me
into a corrupt, wild vine?"
—Jeremiah 2:21

When God's people depart from Him, they do not bear the fruit they were set apart and cultivated to bear.

Jesus declared Himself to be the true vine. Using the language of the vine grower, Jesus described a living union between His disciples and Himself. Just as Jesus is connected to the Father, all followers of Jesus are connected to the Father through their living fellowship with Jesus. The result of this living union is holiness and eternal life (Rom. 6:22). His life flows into our lives and transforms, or changes us, into His likeness. His holiness changes our lives and makes us useful to God, as Jesus' life was useful to the Father.

Holy People Reflect God's Nature

When the world looks at God's vineyard, His people, what do they see? The Bible tells us that God's holiness is so radiant that we cannot look upon His perfect holiness and live. When Moses asked God if he could see Him, God told Moses to go into a crevice of the mountain. As God passed by the crack in the rocks, Moses would be allowed to see no more than the aftermath of His passing—literally, "God's back."

When Moses came down from the mountain, his face shone so brightly that the people were terrified. Moses was reflecting God's glory. Even God's glory must be honored. Moses, at the burning bush, was told to remove his shoes because "the place where you are standing is holy ground" (Exod. 3:5).

Yet it is not only God's glory that we can see in His holiness. There is also the "beauty of holiness." A wonderful description of the beauty of holiness is found in a psalm that is not part of the Book of Psalms. (A psalm is a song, after all, and not all songs are always found in songbooks.) This one is found in 1 Chronicles 16:8–36. In verse 29 of this psalm, David says,

"Give to the LORD the glory due his name;

Bring an offering and come before Him.

Oh worship the LORD in the beauty of holiness!" (NKJV).

God has created the physical beauty of the universe, but the holiness of His character is also the inspired beauty that attracts us to His love. When others see the beauty of God's

---

The wisdom of the prudent is to give thought to their ways,
   but the folly of fools is deception.

—Proverbs 14:8

Our fathers disciplined us for a little while as they thought best; but God disciplines us for our good, that we may share in his holiness. No discipline seems pleasant at the time, but painful. Later on, however, it produces a harvest of righteousness and peace for those who have been trained by it.

—Hebrews 12:10–11

holiness reflected by His people, they will see His love and respond to His holiness.

> "I have given them the glory that you gave me, that they may be one as we are one: I in them and you in me. May they be brought to complete unity to let the world know that you sent me and have loved them even as you have loved me.
>
> —John 17:22–23

Pursue Holiness

One of God's ways is described in John 14:15. "If you love me, you will obey what I command." In this same chapter, Jesus also said, "If anyone loves me, he will obey my teaching" (v. 23).

Man's righteousness only comes from trusting God for salvation. The outgrowth of trust is obedience. Actively obeying God is how we pursue holiness. Living a righteous life sets us apart for God's holy purpose and makes us holy.

The result of the pursuit of holiness is deeds. Becoming more obedient to God results in God's involving us in His activity. James 2:20 says, "Faith without deeds is useless." The same chapter deals with what some argue: that believers have faith and others have deeds (v. 18). However, the answer to that argument is, "Show me your faith without deeds, and I will show you my faith by what I do. You believe that there is one God. Good! Even the demons believe that—and shudder" (vv. 18–19).

Abraham: Faith and Works

As James continues, he says that evidence of true faith produces godly deeds is found in the Old Testament story of Abraham. "Was not our ancestor Abraham considered righteous for what he did when he offered his son Isaac on the altar? You see that his faith and his actions were working together, and his faith was made complete by what he did" (James 2:21–22).

In Abraham, God was looking for someone whose faith would become the pattern for saving faith. God had spoken to Abraham earlier in his life, commanding him to travel to a promised land that God would show him. God also told him that he would give him and his wife a son and make them the parents of nations.

Many more years went by before the promised son was born. But he was born at a time when only God could have caused such an elderly couple to have a baby.

> Make every effort to live in peace with all men and to be holy; without holiness no one will see the Lord.
> —Hebrews 12:14
>
> You are standing here in order to enter into a covenant with the LORD your God, a covenant the LORD is making with you this day and sealing with an oath, to confirm you this day as his people, that he may be your God as he promised you and as he swore to your fathers, Abraham, Isaac and Jacob.
> —Deuteronomy 29:12–13

Abraham's relationship with God was characterized by trust. Trust led to obedience, and obedience led to righteousness, or holiness. What would any man who had been loved with God's perfect love for forty-five years do when God asked him to sacrifice the promised son? Abraham responded with love and trust in God. And God's response to Abraham was to stop him from killing his son. "Do not do anything to him. Now I know that you fear God" (Gen.22:12). Having obeyed God, Abraham was told, "All nations on earth will be blessed, because you have obeyed me" (Gen. 22:18).

Abraham's faith was completed in works. His trust and obedience resulted in holiness. His faith was not dead.

What a Holy God Can Do

It may seem difficult to grasp God's working through all of His people. You might feel overwhelmed to think of yourself as just one in a multitude of believers. Yet sometimes an individual may be where God starts to work among His people, calling for holiness. Then the result may be a response that involves many of God's people. When this happens, it is revival in the truest sense.

And what does God do with people who offer Him their all? He does what only He can do as He takes the commitment of the few and reaches the many. With 120 in the Upper Room (Acts 2) in the first century, God began a work that turned the Roman Empire upside down. With seven young men (among them Adoniram Judson) praying under a haystack during a nineteenth-century thunderstorm, God launched the modern missions movement. It took a twenty-seven-year-old man named Evan Roberts in 1904, letting God shape him and his life of prayer, to see a hundred thousand people in Wales come to know Christ in just six months.

Repentance—Return to the Ideal

Many Christians do not recognize the seriousness of sin. Obedience is not an option for believers—it is a command. Disobedience of God's commands is categorized as sin. Jesus said that believers love Him if they obey Him (John 14:15). Failure to obey directly affects our love relationship with God. Righteousness and holiness in our lives reflects the impact of God's transforming truth on us.

In the First Epistle of John, the Bible says, "If we claim to have fellowship with him yet walk in the darkness, we lie and do not live by the truth. But if we walk in the light, as he is in the light, we have fellowship with one another, and the blood of Jesus, his Son, purifies us from all sin" (1 John 1:7).

So, with sin in our lives, we cannot remain close to God or live holy unto God. We are living a lie. In response, God's way is to deal with sin so severely that we will return to holiness and remain in it. God's discipline is certain because He loves us. The Bible says that God disciplines those He loves (Rev. 3:19). Yet many fear God's discipline because they only think of discipline as punishment. God's desire is to develop us to be more like Him. He did not send His Son to die for our sins to provide more reason to strike us when we fail (Heb.12:5–6).

The Father shows us mercy and desires that, when He deals with sin in our lives, our response will be repentance, the most positive word in the Bible. Repentance, or turning from our sin, goes hand in hand with confession of our sin, admitting that we have disobeyed. Until God disciplines, we may not have realized the extent or effect of our sin. "If we claim to be without sin, we deceive ourselves and the truth is not in us" (1 John 1:8). When confession leads to repentance, we experience the grace of God in action. "If we confess our sins, he is faithful and just and will forgive us our sins and purify us from all unrighteousness" (1 John 1:9).

Holiness Matters

Isaiah the prophet was well educated and a superb writer, as the Book of Isaiah, in the Old Testament, bears witness. He was either a relative or a close friend of King Uzziah and was deeply affected by the king's death. Uzziah had been a good king who came to a tragic end. At, or near, this event, Isaiah's remarkable yielding to be truly God's prophet began.

The temple was where Uzziah's arrogance led him to disobey God and be stricken by God's judgment. Isaiah had loved his king and was broken by Uzziah's disgrace and manner of dying. In his grief Isaiah went into the temple of God. There, Isaiah saw the Lord high and lifted up (Isa. 6:1).

The Hebrew word translated here as "Lord" is *Adonai*, which means "sovereign one." It is not a name, but the title for God. In most translations, when we see the word LORD in small capital letters, this refers to God's Hebrew name, "Yahweh." When we see the word *Lord* capitalized, it refers to God's Hebrew title, "Adonai." The psalmist in Psalm 8:1 said,

> O LORD, our Lord,
>   how majestic is your name in all the earth!

The psalmist actually used God's name and title, "O Yahweh, our Adonai, how excellent is your name in all the earth!"

Isaiah heard God's angels say, "The whole earth is full of his glory" (Isa. 6:3). When God is present, there is no room for anything else. When God spoke, the door posts moved and the house was filled with smoke (6:4) A dedicated, yet sinful man, Isaiah cried out,

> "Woe is me, for I am undone!
> Because I am a man of unclean lips,
> And I dwell in the midst of a people of unclean lips:
> For my eyes have seen the King,
> The LORD of hosts."
>
> —Isaiah 6:5 NKJV

Had Isaiah talked about God for His punishment of Uzziah's disdain for the holiness of God? To the ancient Hebrews the tongue was believed to express the nature of a person, for speech was viewed as the expression of the heart. Use of the tongue had ethical consequences, good and bad. It could be used to honor God or cause separation from God (Ps. 36:1). For whatever reason, Isaiah felt he had dishonored God. Immediately the fire from the altar that Uzziah had unworthily attempted to light was now used by the seraphim to take a live coal from the altar, touch Isaiah's mouth, and cleanse his lips from sin. The message and the truth are clear: like the message of the cross, only the activity of God can touch us at the place of our sin and burn out its cancer with His holiness.

Isaiah had come to the temple because his earthly king was dead. He was confronted with the King of kings, who is eternal. God is sovereign over all of life, and to God holiness matters.

The Ideal

When God restores us to right relationship with Him, the result is removal of sin and a return to righteousness. In Isaiah an incredible picture of restoration is given. God describes what can happen when His people turn to Him. The spiritual condition of God's people even affects what happens to the land they live in. Isaiah, chapter 35, lists the outcome. While nothing is impossible with God, what life can be like for His followers through holiness is astonishing!

> The desert and the parched land will be glad;
>   the wilderness will rejoice and blossom.
> Like the crocus, it will burst into bloom;
>   it will rejoice greatly and shout for joy.
> —Isaiah 35:1–2

The spiritual condition of God's people determines what God will reveal of Himself to them as their Judge and Deliverer (Isa. 35:4). Through holiness the hearts of God's people can bloom like a miracle in the desert.

Repentance: Individual and Corporate

God is looking for holy people through whom He can work in revealing Himself to a watching world. God needs clean vessels. God wants people, families, and churches who will obey and serve Him. "What kind of people ought you to be? You ought to live holy and godly lives as you look forward to the day of God and speed its coming. . . . Make every effort to be found spotless, blameless and at peace with him" (2 Pet. 3:11–12, 14).

Repentance is essential to turn from sin and receive God's forgiveness. Repentance is not only a personal matter,

---

Then will the eyes of the blind be opened
    and the ears of the deaf unstopped.
Then will the lame leap like a deer,
    and the mute tongue shout for joy.
Water will gush forth in the wilderness
    and streams in the desert.
The burning sand will become a pool,
    the thirsty ground bubbling springs.
In the haunts where jackals once lay,
    grass and reeds and papyrus will grow.

And a highway will be there;
    it will be called the Way of Holiness.
The unclean will not journey on it;
    it will be for those who walk in that Way;
wicked fools will not go about on it.

                    —Isaiah 35:5–8

just as sin is not only personal. Repentance, like sin, can be exercised by groups and congregations.

Repentance is the most positive word in the Bible. Repentance is receiving the freedom of forgiveness and restored relationship with God. Psalm 89:15–16 points out that those who walk in the light of God's presence rejoice in His name all day long, exulting in righteousness. What a contrast to a life of rebellion! Walking in the light is easily seen to be preferable to walking in darkness.

Why is it important for believers, their fellowships, and their families to be circumspect about repenting of sin? It is because, in His sovereignty, God has chosen to work through His people to bring about world redemption and spiritual awakening. That is why God is so brokenhearted when His people are not what they ought to be. In such times His people miss out on fullness of life and cannot be used to reach a dying world.

A Lifestyle of Repentance

It is important that God's people never confuse confession with repentance. Many of us recognize the wisdom of admitting our failures and the value of a fresh start. But repentance is a step in a process. Peter warned someone who tried to buy salvation that if the man repented, perhaps God would forgive Him (Acts 8:22). God's forgiveness requires that we turn from sin with a heart that is broken, a heart that sees the effect of its sin, and seeks refuge in God's righteousness. "But the eyes of the LORD are on those who fear him, on those whose hope is in his unfailing love . . . We wait in hope for the LORD; he is our help and our shield" (Ps. 33:18, 22).

But too many people take the commands of God as suggestions. When God spoke through Joshua to the children of Israel, the message was this:

> For I command you today to love the LORD your God, to walk in his ways, and to keep his commands, decrees and laws; then you will live and increase, and the LORD your God will bless you in the land you are entering to possess.
>
> But if your heart turns away and you are not obedient, and if you are drawn away to bow down to other gods and worship them, I declare to you this day that you will certainly be destroyed.
>
> —Deuteronomy 30:16–18a

God assured His people that without obedience they would be destroyed. Not "possibly inconvenienced," or partially inconvenienced, but disobedience would completely destroy them.

Repent When Your Heart Shifts

Repentance and obedience are crucial to living a life that is holy and acceptable to God. If our hearts shift away from God and His holiness, we may not even recognize what has happened and we may neglect repentance.

One way that you can tell that your heart has shifted away from righteousness is that you do not hear clearly from God. "He who belongs to God hears what God says. The reason you do not hear is that you do not belong to God" (John 8:47). The Bible is full of incidents where God spoke and those who were not godly, or who were in rebellion against God, did not hear or recognize the warning or command.

King Saul, of the Old Testament, was one who had often been guided by the Lord but who met his end on the battlefield when he rejected God's guidance. The prophet Samuel spoke God's judgment to Saul. "'You acted foolishly' . . . 'you have not kept the command the LORD your God gave you; if you had, he would have established your kingdom over Israel for all time'" (1 Sam. 13:13).

Saul's departure from holiness finally led him to destruction, instead of to repentance. That may seem harsh, but if we must consider that when someone lacks assurance that God is speaking, God is very gracious to reveal Himself more clearly. Consider the story of Gideon (Judg. 6). God spoke to him through an angel. Gideon, who may have feared the truth more than he actually doubted it, asked for a sign. He prepared a sacrifice, and "the angel of the LORD touched the meat and the unleavened bread. Fire flared from the rock, consuming the meat and the bread. And the angel of the LORD disappeared. When Gideon realized that it was the angel of the Lord, he exclaimed, 'Ah, Sovereign LORD! I have seen the angel of the LORD face to face!'" (Judg. 6:21–22). Gideon was sure God had spoken.

Repent When You Lose the Fear of God

Another barrier to holiness is losing the fear of God. If you know God, it may be hard to imagine forgetting His love and mercy, power or might. Yet the Bible is full of examples of God's people quickly losing their fear of the Almighty. Losing the fear of God leads to the loss of the fear of sin. Losing our fear of sin leads to unrighteousness and the loss of holiness.

The Israelites had seen God deliver them time after time. Often the deliverance was in the form of astounding miracles. Yet when it came time to cross the Jordan River and take the promised land, Moses had to deliver a harsh speech to the people of God. The result of resisting God's command was that no adults (with two exceptions) would live to cross over into the promised land. God commanded them to wander in the desert for decades longer until all the disobedient ones had died (Deut. 1:35–40). He declared that if they disobeyed Him again and tried to enter the land anyway, they would do it without Him and they would be defeated (v. 42). The Israelites repented (v. 45), but God could not be moved. He spared their lives but postponed their destiny to the next generation.

"My son, do not make light of the Lord's discipline,
    and do not lose heart when he rebukes you,
because the Lord disciplines those he loves,
    and he punishes everyone he accepts as a son."
—Hebrews 12:5–6

"Those whom I love I rebuke and discipline. So be earnest, and repent."
—Revelation 3:19

The Israelites were ready to settle down, literally. They felt that things were good enough on the bank of the river. Crossing into the promised land would no doubt lead to more battles, and life seemed fine right where they were. There is a human tendancy to settle for what is good instead of obeying God for what is best.

Repentance for the Individual

Repentance can guide each and every believer to a fresh encounter with God. Each believer can anticipate that God is willing to speak to a clean heart. The Holy Spirit has the assignment to reveal truth and to convict of sin, righteousness, and judgment. Whenever God speaks, He calls for obedience, and your response will have far-reaching consequences. If you want God to speak to you, then you must be prepared to obey Him when He does speak. When God speaks, what you do next reveals what you believe about God. Your actions will present a picture of your faith, or lack of it.

To hear the Creator of the universe speak to you and then refuse to obey is a terrible offense to God. He is your Creator. He is your Lord and Savior. He has every right to be Lord of your life. You need to be prepared to release your life to God's control.

When the Holy Spirit works through the Word of God and brings you face-to-face with God, you are accountable for the relationship. At that point you must either reject Him or obey Him. To sin in ignorance is one thing, but

God judges much more severely those who sin with knowledge of the truth.

Corporate Repentance

Because of God's great love for His people and a lost world, God disciplines His people in love until they return to Him. God has issued a promise to His people. "If my people, who are called by my name, will humble themselves and pray and seek my face and turn from their wicked ways, then will I hear from heaven and will forgive their sin and will heal their land" (2 Chron. 7:14).

Because of His love for His people and the lost world, God disciplines His people, both individuals and congregations, when they are wayward. God's discipline will become more intense until His children cry out to Him, yet God is patient and long-suffering. Like the father of the prodigal son, our heavenly Father waits eagerly for His children to return to Him (John 15:17–24).

Though longsuffering, God does not give options for repentance. Churches, like individuals, can return to Him and His holiness, or face the consequences of sin (1 John 1:9). The exciting part about this process is that positive word *repentance*. God stands ready to receive His people when they return. He cleanses and forgives. He gives a new heart with which to serve Him. He provides the fullness of the Holy Spirit to empower them for His work, and He restores the joy of being in the family of God.

When God has a people rightly related to Him, He is able to display His glory to a watching world. When people experience the mighty power of God bringing wholeness to their lives, others will notice and want a similar experience of life.

Think About—Pray About

You and I have the great possibility of making a difference because God has given us promises that say He will respond when we have responded to Him. We cannot be in the presence of a Holy God and remain the same. We will either be drawn to Him or hardened as we reject Him again and thereby sin against God.

- As extensions of His own Son, the Father cares for His branches with all the love He has for His Son. When we are rooted and grounded in Christ, we are set apart and made holy for God's use and glory. If God loves and cares for you like a gardener tending his vineyard, how do you share His love and care for other believers?

- Abraham knew God. James knew God. Evan Roberts knew God. All of them, because they knew God, also knew what God required of them. Their faith in God kept their relationship with God strong. And God rewarded their faithfulness by building their character. God used the witness of their lives and traveled over them, as His highway of holiness. These believers reflected God's holiness to all around them and all who have come after them. Are you leaving a legacy of holiness?

- Holiness is being like God. Sin is the opposite of holiness. That is because sin is rebellion against God and coming short of what God has required. You might think, *I'm just human,* but you are not! You once were, but now you are the child of the King of kings, indwelled as a temple of God, and your life is not your own. Christ now lives out His life in your life. Consider and pray about this as the reality of life for you as a believer.

- God's people are the body of Christ. The word *corporate* means to be "of the body." If someone has a heart attack, that person's entire body is affected. Likewise, no one would volunteer to run a marathon race while having a toothache or sing a concert while his immune system was fighting the flu. Our bodies are affected by whatever happens to any one of its parts. Are you, as a body part, bringing God's holiness or discipline to the body? Are you demonstrating obedience or rebellion?

CHAPTER 5

The Ways of God Are True

Thomas said to him, "Lord, we don't know where you are going, so how can we know the way?"

Jesus answered, "I am the way and the truth and the life. No one comes to the Father except through me."

—John 14:5–6

GOD IS TRUTH; THEREFORE, every word of God is true and all the ways of God are true. God has revealed, from the beginning of creation to the eventual end of this world, that He is the Creator and Master of everything that we can know to be true. He is the Truth from which all existence comes. God created us and everything else to serve His purpose. He has created the world and everything in it. He has supplied us with physical and spiritual truths that we can know and live by. Because God by His very nature is true, He is never on trial. Everything else is to be understood and judged by Him as the standard of Truth. Every Christian must settle in his own mind and heart that the truth is in God and from God. Therefore, the greatest freedom in the life of the Christian comes from knowing that God is true.

The psalmist spoke of God's Truth many times and in many ways. "As for God, his way is perfect; the word of the Lord is flawless. He is a shield for all who take refuge in him. For who is God besides the LORD and who is the Rock except our God" (Ps. 18:30–31)? God who is true is the very foundation for all that can be, and can be known. His Truth is also the basis by which everything is to be measured!

God not only created all that is real, but He also has promised to destroy and recreate the earth and the heavens. When God reaches the end of His patience, He will close the time for salvation and will judge everyone by his Truth (2 Pet. 3:3–10).

God has put Truth before us so that He will not be hidden from us. Psalm 19:1–2 states,

> The heavens declare the glory of God;
> the skies proclaim the work of his hands.
> Day after day they pour forth speech;
> night after night they display knowledge.

God created the heavens and put into place all the features of our universe. They stand in silent witness, declaring by their presence that God has ordered their existence. Even science continues to confirm the order and pattern of the universe and the symmetry of physics.

Just as there are physical laws, God has given mankind His spiritual laws. He created us with the capacity for justice and His laws.

The precepts of the LORD are right,
> giving joy to the heart.
The commands of the LORD are radiant,
> giving light to the eyes.
>
> —Psalm 19:8

God delivers the universe and mankind from physical and spiritual chaos with His truth.

Truth Is a Person

Jesus is the perfect expression of God. "In the beginning was the Word, and the Word was with God, and the Word was God. He was with God in the beginning" (John 1:1). "The word became flesh"—Jesus is the perfect expression of God—" . . . full of grace and truth" (John 1:14). "Truth came through Jesus Christ" (John 1:17)—real, definite, and absolute, not subjective. At creation—as God spoke and it was so—God spoke the Word of Truth. At the right time, the Word of Truth He spoke became flesh, and it was so.

Whenever God speaks, it is so. "And God said, 'Let the water under the sky be gathered to one place, and let the dry ground appear.' And it was so" (Gen. 1:9). God's Word is more true and certain than the very ground He created. Isaiah 55:10–11 assures you that just as other things you have experienced—rain, snow, sprouting seeds, and the bread that is made from the grain that grows from the seed—so is the word of His mouth.

> It will not return to me empty,
> but will accomplish what I desire
> > and achieve the purpose for which I sent it.

God never speaks except that He intends to accomplish what He says. What God thinks, He does. Isaiah 46:9b–10 says,

> "I am God, and there is no other;
> I am God, and there is none like me.
> I make known the end from the beginning,
>   from ancient times, what is still to come.
> I say: My purpose will stand,
>   and I will do all that I please."

God's Word Is True

God's Word is absolute and True, just as God is. When He speaks, He is already in the process of doing what He spoke. That is why it is important to know His ways and thoughts so that you can recognize and experience Him working in your life. This works hand in hand with faith being a way of God. Our faith is in God, who is Truth. We can trust God because He is literally Truth.

God Expresses Himself as Truth

One of the ways of God is to express Truth. When we are confronted by the truth, we are confronted by God, and this confrontation forces us to reveal the condition of our relationship with God. Jesus was the Truth of God confronting the world. In John 14:6, Jesus says, "I am the way and the truth and the life. No one comes to the Father except through me. If you really knew me, you would know my Father as well. From now on, you do know him and have seen him."

What does it mean that Jesus is the way? As long as you are in relationship to Him, you are dead center in the ways of God. But you cannot call on Him to bless your ways. He *is* your way. And in everything His presence will guide you. You actually only need guidance one step at a time. Most of us say, "Lord, let me see the whole route, and then I'll know where to go." But God says: "All you need is *Me*. And if you do everything that I tell you, one day at a time, you will be dead center where I want you to be. I will not let you know where I am taking you and then let you figure out how to get there. You cannot get there without me. I am your way." So it takes a daily relationship and letting God direct, evaluating our experience against the measure of His truth, as we trust in where He will lead next. God is Truth and will reveal Himself.

The Lord Almighty has sworn,
　　"Surely, as I have planned, so it will be,
　　　　and as I have purposed, so it will stand.
　　　　　　. . . . .
For the LORD Almighty has purposed, and who
　　can thwart him?
　　His hand is stretched out and who can turn it
　　　　back?
　　　　　　　　　　　　　　—Isaiah 14:24, 27

Unbelief Rejects the Truth

Unbelief is not just a slip of character—it is rebellion against God. The implications of unbelief in God are far reaching. Rejecting the truth is treating lightly what God treats seriously. But it is not a minor matter; it is a major matter.

Rejection of truth at any moment affects your family and those who work for or around you. Your rejection of God substitutes your perspective and desires for those of God. It puts you in God's place in your life and destroys faith. Without faith it is impossible to please God. Do not walk by sight and ask God to bless it. As God's truth says, "We live by faith, not by sight" (2 Cor. 5:7).

Sight and faith are opposites because sight acknowledges man's perspective and faith acknowledges God's. Those who come to God must believe that He is, and that what He is is Truth. Jeff Myers has said that the first sign that a nation is self-destructing is that its citizens believe they can decide for themselves what is right and wrong. "Citizens believe they construct their own reality. Truth that is "out there" to be discovered, we are told truth (ultimately reality itself) is created by their own words and actions."[1]

Myers goes on to give an example of the enormous difference it made to one man when he rejected even obvious, physical truth. "Shortly before the explosion of Mount Saint Helens, park rangers tried to evacuate nearby residents. Harry S. Truman (not the president), a long-time resident, refused to leave. He told rangers, 'That mountain has never exploded during my 80 years of life, and it isn't going to explode now.' When the mountain exploded days later, Mr. Truman was buried under an avalanche 500 feet deep."[2]

Mr. Truman sincerely believed that the evidence and the urgency of the rangers, even the smoke and fumes of the awakening volcano were not representative of truth. He may have believed that the rangers were insincere in their belief that he was in danger. Sincerity, however, is never the test of truth. The only truth we know is God. Truth exists because it comes from the One whose nature is true.

Jesus Rebuked Unbelief

Jesus rebuked unbelief because it denies Him. If something is true, that should settle it. But in the thinking of many, that does not always happen. After the miracle of feeding the five thousand, evening had fallen, and Jesus sent His disciples to cross the lake by boat while He went up on the mountain to pray. Wind and waves slowed the disciples' progress, but

---

Jesus answered, "If you want to be perfect, go, sell your possessions and give to the poor, and you will have treasure in heaven. Then come, follow me."

When the young man heard this, he went away sad, because he had great wealth.

Then Jesus said to his disciples, "I tell you the truth, it is hard for a rich man to enter the kingdom of heaven."

—Matthew 19:21–23

they did manage to get a considerable distance from shore within several hours. Then Jesus walked across the water to join them. "When the disciples saw him walking on the lake, they were terrified. 'It's a ghost,' they said, and cried out in fear. But Jesus immediately said to them: 'Take courage! It is I. Don't be afraid'" (Matt. 14:26–27).

Peter's response was to ask Jesus to tell him to come out to Him on the water, which Jesus did. "Then Peter got down out of the boat, walked on the water and came toward Jesus. But when he saw the wind, he was afraid and, beginning to sink, cried out, 'Lord, save me!' Immediately, Jesus reached out his hand and caught him. 'You of little faith,' he said, 'why did you doubt?'" (Matt. 14:29–31).

Peter had received boldness from Jesus' presence. Then, even as he was experiencing the truth of God, he realized that it challenged the limitations he had always known. So he began to doubt God's truth and literally began to sink. Jesus reached out to Peter and saved him, but He rebuked Peter for his unbelief, asking him why he had doubted. They both climbed into the boat, and the wind died down. "Then those who were in the boat worshiped him, saying, 'Truly you are the Son of God'" (Matt. 14:33). When the Truth is revealed, people respond, either with belief or unbelief. But their response does not alter the fact that God and His Word are true.

God's Word Is True

Truth is the key to the surest, happiest, most confident, peaceful way to live. This does not mean that a life based on Truth, the truth of God, will be serene as far as circumstances.

> Do not be deceived: God cannot be mocked. A man reaps what he sows.
>
> —Galatians 6:7

It does mean that the Holy Spirit will confirm in us that it is God who is speaking and convict us of that truth. Circumstances may cause us to doubt, but when God speaks, His word is like a sword, more certain than gravity, and coming straight from His heart with definite results.

A significant moment, one of those divine moments, that happened in 1727, in a place called Herrnhut, located in present day Germany. Count von Zinzendorf had brought to his lands a group of believers known as Moravians. Persecuted and hounded for their strict dependence on the Bible, they found refuge in Herrnhut. Led by the Count, they formed a small colony and church on the Count's estate.

The Moravians knew what it meant to be saved spiritually and physically, and the Word of God became very powerful to them. In all that they read, they saw the need to respond to God's great love. They began to think of the movable temple, the tabernacle, that had been the reminder of God's presence for the Israelites throughout the Exodus. They remembered the altar of incense, where the flame would never go out.

Because the altar of incense was designed by God to represent the prayers of the people that would continually ascend to the throne of God, they asked themselves, "Why is this not true of us? If God desires that the prayers of His people would rise continually, why have we not been praying day and night?

> Jesus . . . looked toward heaven and prayed: . . .
> "Sanctify them by the truth; your word is truth. As you
> sent me into the world, I have sent them into the
> world. For them I sanctify myself, that they too may be
> truly sanctified."
>
> —John 17:1, 17–19

The little Moravian congregation made a commitment to pray twenty-four hours a day, seven days a week. They divided up their families and took turns. Their prayer commitment lasted over a hundred years, unbroken, in prayer.

The Moravians believed God's Word is true, and God began to work on their hearts. They began to sense the need of other parts of Europe. The little group of people felt that when God spoke, they were constrained to go. They sent young men and others to start churches across Europe. They heard of Greenland's not having the gospel. Several couples stepped out and said, in light of the blood of Jesus and the cost of His sacrifice to the Father, "How could we give Him any less than out lives?"

So deep was their impact as they acted on God's Word that the Moravians opened much of the world to a Christian witness. At one point, about fifty years after their forming a church at Herrnhut, they had more missionaries in place than all other mission societies of their day combined.

God even used them to launch the Methodist movement. John Wesley was returning to England from America, discouraged and spiritually depleted. But during a storm at sea, he was face-to-face with the incredible faith of Moravians on board. Wesley came to know and understand God as he never had before. The result was millions being impacted by the gospel and the seeds of the Second Great Awakening in America and subsequent revivals in England and Wales. One congregation, suddenly encountering their God in His Word, and the Truth shook the world in new and mighty ways.

God's Ways Are Revealed in Scripture

What a thrill to be able to open God's Word! Every time I handle the Word of God, every time I open His book, I realize I'm in the presence of the Author. Not only did He make sure it was written down, and not only did He make sure it was preserved accurately, but He also made sure to give us the wonderful Holy Spirit, who is our Teacher, to guide us every time we hear or read the Word of God.

God is very clear on how He intends for His Word to be followed. "Do not add to what I command you and do not subtract from it, but keep the commands of the LORD your God that I give you" (Deut. 4:2). The Holy Spirit is given to reveal the Truth of the Word to us.

God Communicates Truth

Everywhere I go, I find that God is dealing with people. And this comes as no surprise. Peter has told us that God is "not willing that any should perish but that all should come to repentance" (2 Pet. 3:9 NKJV). God is always at work around us. However, our perception of what God is doing may be affected by our circumstances.

In the Book of Job, we are introduced to the young man Elihu (Job 32:2). Job, as you may recall, was the righteous man whose faith was tested by calamity after calamity. After so many personal and financial tragedies, even Job's health was taken. Three of his friends were very interested in determining how all this had come to pass. Job himself could not think of a single reason. Drawn to the scene, Elihu listened and then became angry. He was angry with Job for justifying himself instead of God and with the three friends for not refuting Job, yet condemning him.

In effect, Elihu told the four that he had arrived, hoping to gain some insight and learn more about God from those older and presumably wiser than he. Instead he had heard a lot of conjecture, but no one had spoken the mind of God.

Elihu spoke what he knew about God, starting by answering the complaint we still hear today, "God is no longer speaking to us."

> "Why do you complain to him
>   that he answers none of man's words?
> For God does speak—now one way, now another—
>   though man may not perceive it."
>   —Job 33:13–14

As the older men had complained, Elihu had been moved by the Spirit of Truth to declare to them what they could not see for themselves, in hopes that they would recognize that they had shut themselves off from the Truth God wished to communicate.

> "In a dream, in a vision of the night,
>   when deep sleep falls on men

I warn everyone who hears the words of the prophecy of this book: If anyone adds anything to them, God will add to him the plagues described in this book. And if anyone takes words away from this book of prophecy, God will take away from him his share in the tree of life and in the holy city, which are described in this book.

—Revelation 22:18–19

as they slumber in their beds,
he may speak in their ears
　　and terrify them with warnings,
to turn man from wrongdoing
　　and keep him from pride,
to preserve his soul from the pit,
　　his life from perishing by the sword.
Or a man may be chastened on a bed of pain,
　　with constant distress in his bones,
so that his very being finds food repulsive
　　and his soul loathes the choicest meal. . . .

"Yet if there is an angel on his side
　　as a mediator, one out of a thousand,
　　to tell a man what is right for him,
to be gracious to him and say,
　　'Spare him from going down to the pit;
　　I have found a ransom for him'—. . . .

"Then he comes to men and says,
　　'I sinned, and perverted what was right,
　　but I did not get what I deserved.

He redeemed my soul from going down to the pit,
  and I will live to enjoy the light.'

"God does all these things to a man—
  twice, even three times—
to turn back his soul from the pit,
  that the light of life may shine on him."
                              —Job 33:15–20, 23–24, 27–30

God Communicates His Truth to You

Through Elihu's speech in Scripture, God speaks to us as clearly as He was speaking to Job. We neglect the price of the lessons we waste when we do not hear God speak through our sufferings (vv. 25–27). It may well be that the only time God can find our mouths closed and our minds in neutral is while we are in bed asleep (vv. 15–16). In the Scripture, God often spoke to people in dreams.

God also communicates His Truth to us through our failures. Job 33:17ff. is a grim reminder that our pride can be devastating in the destruction it can bring. God also speaks to us through preservation. Preservation means that God spared you while others around you perished. He saves for a purpose. By protecting you from the pit or the sword, God directs your attention away from what would destroy you and back to the Truth that brings life.

Decades ago, while serving as a missionary in Okinawa, Roy would end each broadcast of our radio ministry with an invitation to call in with questions and requests for prayer or counseling. One night a caller, a military man, asked Roy if he would come to see him. When Roy arrived the next morning, he met the soldier's wife and son. Roy recognized from the uniform that he was part of Special Forces. He also noticed the Congressional Medal of Honor, rarely given, and rarer still to the living.

The soldier's story started in Vietnam. "I had to decide whether to live or die. Everyone in my outfit was dead. I was the only man left alive. I had pulled the charred bodies of the others out of two burning choppers. All the friends I had served with were dead, and I had a broken leg, a broken arm, and a broken back.

"I looked up into the sky, and I said, 'God, I don't know what you are, or who you are, but I'm about to decide whether to try to hang on or die. Would you just let me know if you even exist?'"

The young man said, "Then, God spoke to me. I didn't hear a voice. I don't know what it was, but God said, 'I am God, and I do care for you. I love you. I am going to spare your life, and you are going to find Me.'"

The soldier went on: "I was listening to your message just last night, and suddenly I realized you are the one I need to talk to. Tell me how to find the God that spoke to me in Vietnam."

In just a few moments Roy helped him know how to receive Jesus as his Lord and Savior. "Would you tell my wife?" he asked. She also received Jesus Christ. "Would you tell my son?" Roy told their ten-year-old boy about Jesus, and he opened his heart to the Savior, too. God speaks through preservation. He spared this man's life to save him and use him to win others. That morning an entire family became a witness of His Truth.

God Functions in Truth

God reveals Truth for a purpose because He functions in Truth. It is His desire that we receive His Truth and live our lives by Truth. To help us, God reveals Himself and His ways to us that are true. One word from God gives us truth to live by securely. "All Scripture is God-breathed and is useful for teaching, rebuking, correcting and training in righteousness, so that the man of God may be thoroughly equipped for every good work" (2 Tim. 3:16).

This passage assures us that Scripture is God's Word, literally breathed by Him. The imagery of God's breathing the Scripture reminds us of how God gave us the gift of life through the first man, Adam (Gen. 2:7). Now Paul is reminding young Timothy that Scripture is both reliable in its truth but also absolute as the standard by which man is taught and judged. God, His Word, and Truth to live by are all vitally connected as a way of God for every believer. The most significant prayer of Jesus nailed down for all of us the place of Truth and the Word of God, in every disciple's life. "Sanctify them by the truth; your word is truth. As you sent me into the world, I have sent them into the world. For them I sanctify

---

"Man does not live on bread alone, but on every word that comes from the mouth of God."

—Matthew 4:4

myself, that they too may be truly sanctified" (John 17:17–19).

God Himself "sanctified" us, or sets us apart exclusively for Himself by Truth. "Your word is truth," Jesus prayed. His Word continually "sets us apart" for God. And His Word is Truth because this is God's nature.

Jesus Himself lived His life by God's Word. Jesus echoed the words of Deuteronomy 8:3 when He answered Satan, "Man does not live on bread alone, but on every word that comes from the mouth of God" (Matt. 4:4). You may be thinking, *Sure, we need the spiritual as well as the physical in order to survive.* But the point here, and throughout God's Word, is that life is more than our bread, and God's Word is more than spiritual guidance. God's Word is life itself, eternal life. When God speaks: (1) it is true; (2) it guides us to life from God; (3) it brings fullness of life when we believe and obey every word from God.

After God had spoken His law to His people through Moses, He said, "They are not just idle words for you—they are your life" (Deut. 32:47). God functions by the words He gives. Our existence, both now and throughout eternity, is determined by God's Word. God's Word is Truth, and because it is, it brings life. It brings His fullness of life to our lives. It is also true that when God sent His Son, every word from His Son brought life.

God Does Not Alter His Truth

The truth of God's ways does not change as it is applied, and we cannot change it (Matt. 24:35). God is Truth, and His nature never changes. Just as Truth by its nature is unchanging, unless God intervenes, so are the consequences of defying God's truth. This unchanging nature of God, when He speaks, gives great joy and confidence in every promise God has spoken.

The tragedy of changing God's Word is clearly seen in the life of King Saul. It cost him his kingdom, his life, and his family. Saul had been chosen by God and anointed by the prophet Samuel to be the first Israelite king (1 Sam. 9:17). Saul was humble but open in trusting God to guide him in leading the people (1 Sam. 9:21). God transformed him and empowered him to serve God as king of his people (1 Sam. 10:6). God's Spirit is His provision, both to know and to do His word.

However, Saul's reign, year after year, was of bitter war (1 Sam. 14:52). But rather than draw closer to God, Saul, by choice, changed, and his heart turned away from God. For example, God had commanded Saul to destroy one of Israel's enemies, the Amalekites, and take no prisoners or plunder (1 Sam. 15:3). But Saul did not trust the truth of

---

"I have come that they may have life, and have it to the full."

—John 10:10b

I have been crucified with Christ and I no longer live, but Christ lives in me. The life I live in the body, I live by faith in the Son of God, who loved me and gave himself for me.

—Galatians 2:20

what God had commanded. He disobeyed, took the enemy king captive, and saved the best of the livestock. "But Saul and the army spared Agag and the best of the sheep and cattle, the fat calves and lambs—everything that was good. These they were unwilling to destroy completely, but everything that was despised and weak they totally destroyed" (1 Sam. 15:9).

Saul and those under his command were now in defiance of God. "Then the word of the LORD came to Samuel: 'I am grieved that I have made Saul king, because he has turned away from me and has not carried out my instructions'" (1 Sam. 15:10). To disobey God's Word is to turn away from Him. To reject God's Word when He speaks is to reject Him. To reject Him is to turn away from Life, the only Life there is.

"When Samuel reached him, Saul said, 'The LORD bless you! I have carried out the LORD's instructions'" (1 Sam. 15:13). Saul's defiance of God's Truth had led to lies, the complete opposite of Truth. Saul tried to alter what God wanted and argued with the truth. "Saul answered, 'The soldiers brought them from the Amalekites; they spared the best of the

---

"Does the LORD delight in burnt offerings and sacrifices
    as much as in obeying the voice of the LORD?
To obey is better than sacrifice,
    and to heed is better than the fat of rams.
For rebellion is like the sin of divination,
    and arrogance like the evil of idolatry.
Because you have rejected the word of the LORD,
    he has rejected you as king."
                                    —1 Samuel 15:22–23

sheep and cattle to sacrifice to the LORD your God, but we totally destroyed the rest'" (1 Sam. 15:15).

Samuel stopped Saul and told him that by rejecting God's command he had rejected God, and this cost him his kingdom. It would ultimately cost him his life and the lives of his sons. Samuel told him how serious his rejection of God's word was to God. "To obey is better than sacrifice," and "rebellion is like the sin of divination [witchcraft], and arrogance like the

---

When he had finished washing their feet, he put on his clothes and returned to his place. "Do you understand what I have done for you?" he asked them. "You call me 'Teacher' and 'Lord,' and rightly so, for that is what I am. Now that I, your Lord and Teacher, have washed your feet, you also should wash one another's feet. I have set you an example that you should do as I have done for you. I tell you the truth, no servant is greater than his master, nor is a messenger greater than the one who sent him. Now that you know these things, you will be blessed if you do them."

—John 13:12–17

"A new commandment I give you: Love one another. As I have loved you, so you must love one another. By this all men will know that you are my disciples, if you love one another."

—John 13:34–35

"This is my command: Love each other."

—John 15:17

evil of idolatry. Because you have rejected the word of the LORD, he has rejected you as king" (1 Sam. 15:22–23). God did not give a suggestion to Saul but a command. This command was Saul's life.

Experiencing the Perfect Love of God

Functioning in Truth, living by the Truth, is the only way to life. For example, in the Sermon on the Mount, Jesus said, there are only two ways in life: a narrow way that leads to life and a broad way that leads to death (Matt. 7:13–14). He also said in a startling, but true, word, "few find it." Truth is the one way to life. Once you acknowledge Truth, doing what is contrary to the will of God is sin. One of the conditions of sin is lawlessness. That means to live without law to guide you. In contrast to functioning in Truth, it means living a deadly lie.

A believer must function according to what God says in His Word, because it is absolute Truth. So when the Scripture says to forgive, it means that for the Christian forgiveness is not an option. It is a mandate. God says, if you will not forgive, I will not forgive you (Matt. 6:14–15).

You cannot say, "It is absolutely true that God has said He will forgive me and I will be forgiven, but God did not truly mean it when He said, 'Forgive men when they sin against you.'" To say that not only defies logic; it blasphemes the truth of God.

God Cannot Lie

Even though the Truth of God has been given to us, we easily misrepresent the Truth of God, turning the Truth of

God into a lie. We take the Truth of God and put it into our own words and alter it just enough to make it our way and a lie. God, who is Truth, is the One who does not lie. That is how the prophet Samuel described God (1 Sam. 15:29). What a clear statement of who God is! His way is Truth, so He does not lie. Lying is something that people do. Numbers 23:19a says, "God is not a man, that he should lie, nor a son of man, that he should change his mind." The result of being and speaking Truth is that God does not deceive us or abandon us. When God speaks, it is already accomplished. "Does he speak and then not act? Does he promise and not fulfill? I have received a command to bless; he has blessed, and I cannot change it" (Num. 23:19b–20). God does not lie. God is Truth, and His way is truth.

Lying Is Natural—for Man

The human condition is a desperate one. The psalmist, who was quoted by the apostle Paul, described how we appear to God.

> "'There is no one righteous, not even one;
>   there is no one who understands,
>   no one who seeks God.
> All have turned away,
>   they have together become worthless;
> there is no one who does good,
>   not even one. . . .
>   "Their mouths are full of cursing and bitterness.
> Their feet are swift to shed blood;

ruin and misery mark their ways,

and the way of peace they do not know.

There is no fear of God before their eyes.'"

—Romans 3:10–12, 14–18.

We are disoriented to the ways of God. We naturally find it hard to trust Him, preferring to trust ourselves. We cannot believe His ways and, instead, we function in bitterness and hatred, or with lack of faith in the truth. Lack of faith simply says we do not believe God. So, when we do not exercise faith, we do not accommodate ourselves to God. Instead, we ask Him to accommodate Himself to us.

God knows that lying, like all sin, comes naturally to man. That is why God gave us His law. God wants us to know His way of truth. Observing God's law does not make us righteous, though it gives us a chance to achieve compliance. The law makes us conscious of sin, but God wants more from us than righteous behavior. God wants each of us to become righteous. Only the indwelling Truth of God provides us with God's righteousness. Only salvation through His Son Jesus Christ will bring truth into our hearts and make us righteous in God's sight.

No one who practices deceit
will dwell in my house;
no one who speaks falsely
will stand in my presence.

—Psalm 101:7

God Does Not Change

We have already seen in 2 Timothy 3:14–16 that all Scripture is God-breathed—straight from God who is Truth. The Scripture declares that it is useful for "training in righteousness." Knowing the truth of God literally trains us in

> The prayer of a righteous man is powerful and effective.
> —James 5:16

righteousness. We have received training in many things over our lifetime. We rely on people whom we believe have been trained to do what we are trusting them to do. We trust physicians to know medicine, contractors to know how to build, pilots to know how to fly planes or guide ships. It is natural for us to trust the training of others as long as they seem to be doing their jobs. Yet, why is it difficult sometimes to trust the Truth and the fact that it can train us in righteousness?

> There is a way that seems right to man,
> but in the end it leads to death.
>
> —Proverbs 16:25

Without training in the truth, we have no chance of finding the way that leads to life. Ask any number of people who have become rich or famous, or who have achieved world records of one kind or another. Did they find the way of life through their celebrity status, money, or achievements? Will publicity or wealth answer the needs of their hearts? Do people sometimes respond to those things as if they will? Unlike the truth of God, fame is fleeting, money can be lost, and achievements forgotten. They do not last, and they are not trustworthy. Only God, who is Truth, is eternal.

You Can Trust Truth

The ways of God are not on trial. Everything that comes from the mouth of God is true. Anything else leads to death and destruction. Anything that differs from the way of God is error. When Truth enters your life, the result is fruitfulness (Matt. 13:23). When lies are directing your life, the result is ruin.

You are probably aware when using a computer that what you enter, whether on the screen or through the software, determines what result you will get. A comma instead of a period in a computer address can keep you from reaching that site. The wrong format or kind of program in any format or program that is incompatible with your computer setup will halt your search. You will never achieve your desired results without the right data.

Electricity illustrates the truth of God's ways. Electricity does not change. Millions of people make enormous use of this power source every day. Use electricity according to its laws, and you have light and comforts and conveniences of all kinds. Electrical power even saves lives, powering hospitals and medical equipment of all kinds. But failure to observe the laws brings death instead of life. That is the truth of electricity. Likewise, follow God's way of truth, and you will have life that lasts forever. Truth is a way of God.

Truth Sets You Free

One of the most radical revelations Christ made about Himself is found in John 14:6: "'I am the way and the truth and the life. No one comes to the Father except through me.'" In this verse, Jesus didn't say, "I'll show you the way," or "I know the truth and will tell it to you," or, "I can heal you and give you a better life." Rather, He said that He *is* the Way, the Truth, and the Life.

Thomas, one of Jesus' disciples, had asked Jesus, "Lord, we don't know where you are going, so how can we know the way?" (John 14:5). Jesus' answer was, "I am the way." In the Moffat translation of the Bible, Jesus' answer is translated, "I am the true and living way." Centuries before, the psalmist had prayed, "Teach me thy way, O LORD, and I will walk in your truth. Give me an undivided heart, that I may fear your name" (Ps. 27:11, Ps. 80:11 KJV). Many who were seeking God had asked this same question, over and over.

Jesus did not offer to open the way, or point out the way, and hope that those following it would not get lost. Jesus comes to live in us and guide us. He will not let us get lost. He is as spiritually present in the hearts of believers as He was physically present in the boat with Thomas. When Christ is present, the truth of every situation differs from purely human perceptions.

Free from Fear and Hopelessness

Jesus fell asleep in the boat. A sudden and ferocious storm arose. To the disciples' human understanding, considering the

"For if you forgive men when they sin against you, your heavenly Father will also forgive you. But if you do not forgive men their sins, your Father will not forgive your sins."

—Matthew 6:14–15

storm, the strength of their vessel, and their ability to sail under such conditions, they were certain they would soon sink. They were frantic! But the truth of the situation was not what they thought. The Truth of the situation was asleep in the boat! The reality of Christ's presence made, and makes, all the difference. "Then he got up and rebuked the winds and the waves, and it was completely calm" (Matt. 8:26).

What was the truth in the death of Lazarus as recorded in John 11? From the world's perspective, not only was Jesus' friend Lazarus dead, but his body had begun to decompose. From the world's perspective there was no hope. But when the Truth arrived, He commanded, "Lazarus, come out!" and His friend stepped forth, raised from the dead. Did the presence of Christ make a difference in the truth of the situation? Absolutely!

How about those who had been blind or lame since birth and were made whole by Christ? From the world's perspective their situations were hopeless. But in Christ, in Truth, the reality of the situation was completely the opposite. They were not only able to see and walk, but they could now more effectively proclaim the glory of Christ to a watching, astonished world.

According to Christ's disciples, the truth of the situation dictated that they ought to send the thousands of people away to the towns and villages to buy food after a long day of listening to the Master (Matt. 14:15–21). After all, the only food they could find was two small fishes and five loaves of bread. Was the truth that the people would starve? No. You can never really know the truth of the situation until you have checked with the One who *is* Truth. When Truth spoke, the reality of the situation was shown to be dramatically different. More than five thousand were fed, and twelve baskets of leftover bread were collected. Kingdom realities rarely mesh with the world's reality.

How can you possibly know the truth of any situation without checking first with the real Truth? You cannot. The world's perspective on any situation is suspect because the world does not understand the truth, and neither will the world understand your faith in Christ who is Truth.

Free from Idolatry

Idols are still a danger among Christians. An idol is anything that takes God's place in your life. Almost anything can serve as an idol, including intangibles such as pride and tangibles such as cars or homes. Idol worship was a frequent problem for many people in the Bible, and some of the descriptions there provide strong insights as to how people create idols.

Paul said that even though God's eternal power and divine nature are obvious in creation, mankind has foolishly exchanged the glory of God for images made to look like mortal man and animals (Rom. 1:22–26). Jeremiah quotes God as saying the things people make to worship, even when they cover them in silver and gold, are no more than scarecrows in a melon patch when the idols are set up and worshiped (Jer. 10:1–5). God expressed what sounds like amazement at being compared to something men can make and also that a man who cannot afford an offering will use the finest materials he can find when he decides to make his own god (Isa. 40:18 20). The height of absurdity is that people will cry out to something they have made, which they know is lifeless, and ignore God who knows all things and has saved them from their troubles (Isa. 46:5–9).

Look carefully at the process: (1) People take something God has made, such as wood; (2) they fashion it into an image of their choosing; (3) they lay over it gold and silver and make it look beautiful; (4) they set it up before them; (5) they begin to worship what their hands have made, depending on "it" to help them and save them; (6) they call out to it, but it has no ears to hear.

We are in danger of doing the same thing with God's Word: (1) We take what God has said; (2) we fashion and change it to meet out desires; (3) we "decorate" it with fancy words and phrases of our own making; (4) we then trust in the word of God we have changed and expect God to bless what we have fashioned. An example would be to say we should love one another but there are exceptions. What God speaks and reveals is the truth. We cannot change His truth and expect God to work.

Free to Forgive As You Have Been Forgiven

As we have already said, you are lying if you announce, "It is absolutely true that God has said He will forgive me and I will be forgiven, but God did not truly mean it when He said, 'Forgive men when they sin against you.'" To say that not only defies logic, but it also blasphemes the truth of God. Forgiveness not only sets you free from your sins, but it can also bring life in the most personal way, through grace, to you and to all those around you.

In 1964, Billy Graham went to Tokyo for the first time. His messages were translated by the Japanese evangelist Hatori. Seeing them preaching in English and Japanese was as

---

"The one who received the seed that fell among the thorns is the man who hears the word, but the worries of this life and the deceitfulness of wealth choke it, making it unfruitful."

—Matthew 13:22

---

one motion, so seamless and graceful, as the gospel was proclaimed to the hushed crowd in an auditorium in Tokyo.

As Billy Graham preached, he would point his finger and say, "It's you the Lord is speaking to tonight. You need Jesus as your Lord and Savior. God is talking to you tonight."

Way up in the balcony was a businessman. He was Dutch by nationality, though he had been raised in Indonesia. Before World War Two, Indonesia was a Dutch colony where he had headed a major oil company's Indonesian operation. When the Japanese invaded, the Dutch government ordered the businessman to burn the oil fields and storage tanks, and to destroy everything that might fuel the Japanese war effort. The government also ordered the citizens to fight to the death to delay the islands' fall to the Japanese. Then the message came to avoid any further loss of life and to surrender.

The businessman was among those taken in a grueling, forced march to a prison camp on the River Kwai. Every morning meant another day of walking in the swift-running river water to conceal the tracks of the exodus of prisoners. They had to walk across the river to determine who was strong enough to work. The weak gave up and were drowned. Those who were too weak to walk in the strong current drowned, sometimes just letting the river carry them away to their deaths. The businessman lost his brothers, his mother, and father, and eventually, every member of his family. But he resolved to live through it. When the prison camp was liberated, though thin and weak, he insisted on joining the invasion of Indonesia, where he helped retake the islands.

When the war was over and prosecution for war crimes began, the businessman went to Tokyo to testify against the commanders of the prison camp on the River Kwai. He was an impressive chief witness. He spoke several languages, including Japanese, and had an incredible memory for dates and atrocities, reciting the names and ranks of every official involved.

After the trials the businessman was asked by the Dutch government to stay in Tokyo as their liaison with the Japanese.

In 1964, he was still working in Tokyo. Somehow, he came to be in the balcony of the auditorium where the Graham Crusade was being held. "Billy Graham's finger was like a cannon pointing to me alone," he said. When the man made his way down from his seat, another man, a former colonel in the Japanese army, was also making his way forward. They were met by one of the counselors at the crusade, a U.S. Air Force colonel, who helped them deal with and accept Jesus Christ as his Lord and Master.

Though not a prison camp officer, the Japanese man had fought on several battlefields against allied forces. Together, in quick succession, both men accepted Christ as Savior. The former enemies threw their arms around each other. I later had the joy and privilege of having both men as deacons when I pastored Tokyo Baptist Church.

Think About—Pray About

- If you will acknowledge the promises of God by operating with confident expectation, you will experience tremendous freedom. It is the freedom that comes from recognizing that God is true, and reliable, and trustworthy. He will do what He has said He will do, in His timing and in His way. Pray according to your

---

We are therefore Christ's ambassadors, as though God were making his appeal through us. We implore you on Christ's behalf: Be reconciled to God.

—2 Corinthians 5:20

faith in Truth as a person, the person of God, and enjoy the freedom that comes from trust in Him.

- God has used many men and women to bring Truth. Take a moment to read 2 Corinthians 5:20. Notice that it says that believers are ambassadors of Christ "as though God were making his appeal through us." Ask God to help you understand the impact of Truth. Ask God to show you how you can be used by living out truth in your life and world.

- God functions in truth. God's truth includes the fact that He loves us and has given us His Word. He deals with us in perfect, consistent love. If God lives in you, how should you function: according to yourself, or according to the truth?

- God is Truth. He has recorded His nature and His ways in His Word and reveals them to us. To go contrary to the ways of God is to go contrary to Him. And to depart from Him is to depart from life. Even the slightest departure is departure, and God will not function contrary to His ways.

- God is Truth. Two men who had been saved from different cultures, taught by experience to hate each other, were made brothers in Christ and became the best of friends. Because God functions in Truth, both were brought together as the Word of God was applied to their lives. God spoke to their hearts, convicting them that there was more to life than what they had lived through. They heard God speak and responded to the truth. Who is near you that God may have prepared to hear and respond to the truth today? Remember, God is not only Truth, He functions in Truth.

1.   Jeffrey L. Myers, "Recognizing the Signs of the Times," http://homeschool.crosswalk. com/myers, 16 May 2000.
2.   Ibid.

CHAPTER 6

The Ways of God Are Eternal

"I am the Alpha and the Omega, the First and the Last, the Beginning and the End."
—Revelation 22:13

A NUMBER OF YEARS AGO, Roy pastored a church in a small Texas town that depended for its livelihood on a huge local ranch. Nearly everyone in the community worked for the ranch or was in a business supported by the ranch. People liked the ranch. Everyone felt like family. And for the most part it was a calm, secure time to live there.

One of the men in the town was lovingly called Uncle Will. He was really no one's uncle but an old bachelor cowboy who had spent nearly all his life working cattle. When I came as pastor of the church, Uncle Will was in his early eighties and still on the payroll at the ranch. He was painfully broken in body and had not been able to do any ranch work for years. But he had survived many falls, broken bones, stampedes, and lonely nights on the open plains to arrive at this time of life.

Uncle Will was not a Christian but was always open to a visit and a discussion about salvation. We became friends, and my wife and I visited him regularly. He told me that his mother had been a Christian and had loved the Lord. She had been a regular church attender, too. As I read the Bible to him, he would acknowledge the truth of God's love offered through His Son, Jesus. Yet Uncle Will would never ask Jesus to forgive him of his sins and become the Lord of his life.

Uncle Will developed a quick-growing cancer and soon became critically ill. We visited him every week and talked to him about his relationship to God. He would acknowledge the truths about salvation and his need for Christ, yet he would not let Christ into his life. His condition steadily worsened.

One morning I received a call from the hospital. Uncle Will was near the end and said he would like to see me.

I consider everything a loss compared to the surpassing greatness of knowing Christ Jesus my Lord, for whose sake I have lost all things. I consider them rubbish, that I may gain Christ and be found in him, . . . I want to know Christ and the power of his resurrection and the fellowship of sharing in his sufferings, becoming like him in his death, and so, somehow, to attain to the resurrection from the dead.

—Philippians 3:8, 10

He seemed to be glad that I had come. Once again I went over God's plan of salvation. Once again he said that he was not ready to receive Jesus as his Savior. I asked him to reconsider. He looked at me, and a chill seemed to come over his body. His eyes turned hard, and he looked away. He said, "No, no, I don't want God now or ever!" He would not look at me and refused to talk. I prayed for him and pleaded with him to open his heart. As I left, I heard him say again, "No, no, no, I don't need God." He died that night, still separated from God, as far as I know. I thought of Proverbs 29:1:

> A man who remains stiff-necked after many rebukes
>   will suddenly be destroyed—without remedy.

Uncle Will had run out of time.

For Eternity, Not Time

God created us for eternity, not for time. Therefore, we live for eternity, not time. The rest of the existence God has granted us extends from now through death and continues for all eternity. God is not limited by time. As the Creator of time, God is not contained by it or limited by it. "I am the Alpha and the Omega, the First and the Last, the Beginning and the End" (Rev. 22:13). God was before time, is now, and will be after time has passed away. Rather than being bound by the chronology we know, God completely surrounds and contains time, not vice versa.

God created us and placed us in time so that we would have opportunity to know Him and come into relationship with Him. He even says that He delays the coming of the end of the world so that more will have opportunity to know Him and be saved (2 Pet. 3:9). God's sense of timelessness is just the opposite of what humans might think. Without the limits of time, someone might think, *What's the hurry?* But God created time and knows how much there is and when the time for eternal remedies will be over.

First Peter 4:7–8 conveys this urgency as a way of shaping the perspective of believers, an urgency many find easy to overlook today. "The end of all things is near. Therefore be clear minded and self-controlled so that you can pray. Above all, love each other deeply, because love covers over a multitude of sins."

This sense of urgency helps us build an eternal perspective. It reminds us that we have little time here, yet what we do affects all eternity. So the admonition is given to be clear minded and self-controlled so that we can pray. When we pray, we communicate with the One who made time and with whom we will spend eternity. Our communication with Him guides us in pointing others to Him. We are told to love one another so that we do not waste the time that we have to work together. An eternal perspective, instead of a time perspective, points us to what is lasting and away from earthly distractions. Loss of self-control and failure to love only diminish what we are able to do and appreciate for the One who is eternal, and with whom we will live for all eternity.

Living Out an Eternal Perspective

I have watched many Christians go absolutely to pieces when they lost a child or a parent to death. The pain is real, but even more so is the consolation. The Holy Spirit is our Comforter, and heaven belongs to those who serve the living God. The watching world says, "I thought Jesus was the resurrection and the life. I guess He wasn't, because I never saw Him being that to you in your grief." Jesus said that He is glorified in those who believe in Him. So, when Jesus makes a statement about who He is, you must decide whether He is telling the truth and whether you will believe Him and allow the world to see that truth through your life.

Are you living your life with an eternal perspective—living out what God has said because you have heard him and you believe Him? Do your actions show a time perspective or an eternal perspective in how you live? How do you treat others? What of your absolute integrity and righteousness? Are you giving a picture of eternal truth at work by the way you live in time?

If you talk about Jesus, you had better live what you talk, or you can blur in time what people should be seeing of eternity. For instance, does Jesus forgive? Jesus forgave even when the offender was absolutely wrong. Did Jesus stand there and justify Himself when He was wrongly accused on so many occasions? You and I might have a tendency to do exactly that. Yet when Jesus was falsely accused, His response said, "I'm secure. I know who I am and whose I am. So now I have the capacity to forgive you."

We want to justify ourselves, and Jesus never did. He lived for eternity, simply living out forgiveness. Was Jesus ever wronged? All the time. Will you ever be wronged? Of course. If you are falsely accused, what will you do? Go to your lawyer, get all the evidence you can, and sue someone? Jesus did not do that. So how will a watching world know the difference that Jesus makes, and how Jesus forgives? When you find yourself in a situation and act like Jesus instead of like the world, you are a witness to the ways of God, and God is glorified. When people say, "I don't understand how you can be that way," you can reply, "I can tell you why. Because my Lord is One who forgives. I also forgive with His enabling, even when I am completely wronged." Will God vindicate His own? Yes. God always vindicates His own and upholds their integrity.

> For the power of the wicked will be broken,
> but the Lord upholds the righteous.
>   —Psalm 37:17

When God vindicates us, it is by His own ways instead of anything we can manipulate. He will let the world know the difference He makes, and He rewards our faithfulness by confirming His truth.

Eternal Truths and Complete Control of Time

If your perspective is mired in time, you could miss how God is acting for eternity throughout time, which He completely controls. On a Wednesday night during prayer meeting, the congregation was making a list of people who needed prayer. After each name we put the name of the person who would call or visit that one for whom we were praying. One man was put on the list, and no one volunteered to contact him. He was a man who did not know God, known for his hard disposition, crude language, and overwhelming size. People were afraid of him.

I already knew the man because his wife had been a member of our church. I met him the night I received a message that the woman had been in an accident and was at the hospital. I arrived at her bedside just as she died. Her husband was in a state of shock. But he would not allow me to offer any words of comfort and left the hospital.

At the funeral he was impassive and accepted sympathy from no one. When I visited his home, he made clear that I was not welcome. Now, nearly a year later, someone was burdened for this man, but no one was willing to visit him. So I said that I would.

Driving home, I had to pass the mobile home where he lived. I was praying about stopping and visiting with him. God had put him on my heart, but the man had made clear that I would not be welcome to try to share the gospel again. When I got to the trailer, I was relieved to see that it was dark. I was sure a well-lit house would have been a sign from God that I should stop. I wanted to accept darkness to mean the opposite.

Glancing up in my rearview mirror, I saw a sliver of light in an end window. I drove on, debating whether seeing that sliver of light was a direction from God. I finally turned around, because I knew what God wanted me to do, regardless of the lights.

I knocked on the door and heard the gruff question, "What do you want?" I told him who I was and asked if he had time for a visit. He asked me to wait. A moment later the trailer began to rock as the man walked to the door—six foot six, three hundred pounds. He let me in as I apologized for the late hour. But I told him that his name had come up in our prayer requests that very night, and I felt that God wanted me to stop by and visit him.

He looked stunned, then began to weep. Through his tears he said, "Today is the anniversary of my marriage. All day long I have been alone, remembering my wife, and how much I love her and miss her." He said, over and over, his wife had told him how much God loved him. He said he had been remembering her words all day and had asked God to send somebody to show him the way to know God.

He looked at me and said, "God sent you to me tonight, Preacher. Please help me find God! I want to live for Him and go to be with my wife in God's heaven when I die."

That night illustrates the eternity that we all will enter and the question of how we will spend it—a question that must be answered on earth. Consider Matthew 25:34, which says, "Then the King will say to those on his right, 'Come, you who are blessed by my Father; take your inheritance, the kingdom prepared for you since the creation of the world.'" God's desire is to prepare us for eternity. He wants us to spend eternity with Him. God Himself is eternal by nature; therefore, His ways are eternal.

Eternal Life Is a Relationship to a Person

When God gives you eternal life, He gives you Himself and a relationship with Him and to His Son. John 17:3 says, "Now this is eternal life: that they may know you, the only true God, and Jesus Christ, whom you have sent." Eternal life is a relationship to a person.

The Greek word for truth is the noun *aletheia*. It refers to truth as distinguished from falsehood and the real distinguished from the unreal and counterfeit. Jesus is the embodiment of the perfect truth of God. He is the personification of the word and wisdom of God. John said, "We beheld His glory, the glory as of the only begotten of the Father, full of grace and truth" (John 1:14 KJV). Jesus is the reliability, trustworthiness, faithfulness, and fidelity of God incarnate. Jesus' character and teaching have no defects. His truth is correct, consistent, and clear.

Another side of eternal truth is the moral over and against the immoral. Jesus said, "This is the verdict: Light has come into the world, but men loved darkness instead of light because their deeds were evil. Everyone who does evil hates the light, and will not come into the light for fear that his deeds will be exposed. But whoever lives by the truth comes into the light, so that it may be seen plainly that what he has done has been done through God" (John 3:19–21).

The apostle John said in 1 John 1:5–6, "This is the message we have heard from him and declare to you: God is light; in him there is no darkness at all. If we claim to have fellowship with him yet walk in the darkness, we lie and do not live by the truth." The darkness of sin has no part in God's truth, and His own character sets the standard for what is right. He hates what is evil. His eternal purpose is seen by His working in the world to overcome evil with His righteousness. The reality of God is eternal truth and light. A relationship is available to us, eternally by God's grace. Jesus is full of grace and truth (John 1:4), and He is the source of grace and truth to us (John 1:17).

One of the most beautiful expressions of Jesus as God's eternal Truth available to us in an eternal relationship with Him is this: "I tell you the truth, whoever hears my word and believes him who sent me has eternal life and will not be condemned; he has crossed over from death to life" (John 5:24). What a promise! This is an eternal truth from the eternal Truth, concerning eternal life, available through an eternal relationship with Jesus Christ.

The Eternal Relationship

I have been reading for many years of the great Shantung Revival in China. In the early twentieth century, this revival began among Southern Baptist missionaries. They were a large part of a group of Westerners gathered in Shantung by the Chinese government during a time of civil strife. Many of the Westerners were missionaries, reluctant to leave the land and people to whom they had been called to witness. During the separation from their mission fields, they began to pray for revival among all believers in China, themselves included. Their response to God's eternal truth deepened their relationship with Him and spread the gospel deeper into China before all missionaries were expelled and churches suppressed later in the century.

A Lutheran missionary nurse from Norway was one of the believers seeking God among those gathered at Shantung. Her name was Marie Munson. Anybody she met would face the question, "Have you ever been born again by the Spirit of the living God?" And if one of them said, "Oh, yes. I have been born again," she would look them straight in the eye and say, "Tell me the clear evidence that this transaction has taken place."

It is recorded that she made no exceptions on the mission field. There was a Chinese evangelist who for ten years had been preaching the gospel. Marie Munson took him aside and asked, "Have you ever been born again by the Spirit of God?" He said, "Why certainly. I am preaching the gospel. I have been for ten years. And people have been

All these people were still living by faith when they died. They did not receive the things promised; they only saw them and welcomed them from a distance. And they admitted that they were aliens and strangers on earth. People who say such things show that they are looking for a country of their own. If they had been thinking of the country they had left, they would have had opportunity to return. Instead, they were longing for a better country—a heavenly one. Therefore God is not ashamed to be called their God, for he has prepared a city for them.

—Hebrews 11:13–16

saved." Marie said, "You didn't hear my question. I asked if you have ever been born again by the Spirit of God." And he answered, "But I am a preacher of the gospel."

In Matthew 7:22, that's the kind of answer that some people gave in a parable about the judgment. So she asked him again, "Can you tell me clearly the evidence that you have been born again by the Spirit of the living God?" The evangelist walked away in anger. But the next day, he returned, an absolutely broken servant of God. "I was angry with you over what you asked me. But the question haunted me. Last night I asked myself, *Have I ever been born again by the Spirit of the Living God? What evidence is there in my life that this has ever taken place?*"

He continued. "I began to look though my life, and everything that I saw that ought to have been there was missing. There was never a time when the old passed away. There was never a time when everything became new," he said, turning to the diminutive missionary nurse. "I want you to know that last night I cried out to God and was born again for the first time by the Spirit of the living God. Now I know that He is my Lord." Then he said, "For ten years I have lived under false pretenses and I have taken the support and the offerings of the people of God. I am going to stand and tell the people of God that I have done this. From now until the end of my ministry I will never again take a cent from any of God's people."

That evangelist played an integral part as God brought revival to Shantung. Ten times as many people came to faith in Jesus Christ from this born-again evangelist than had responded in the previous years when he was preaching truth from an unchanged heart. Now he had an eternal relationship with the eternal ways and truth of God.

If anyone has entered into a union with Christ, he is a new creation. The old things have passed away, and everything has become new (2 Cor. 5:17). That is the eternal difference that God makes when anyone comes into relationship with Him.

If you have been looking for something to transform you, but have not seen it in your life or if you have watched God transform others and asked yourself if there is more to serving God than attending meetings, the resounding answer from heaven is yes! There is new life in Jesus Christ.

Be reminded that wherever sin abounds grace from God will be much more abounding. Ephesians 3:16–19 describes the relationship awaiting anyone who will move beyond head knowledge or arguments and enter an eternal relationship with the living God.

> I pray that out of his glorious riches he may strengthen you with power through his Spirit in your inner being, so that Christ may dwell in your hearts through faith. And I pray that you, being rooted and established in love, may have power, together with all the saints, to grasp how wide and long and high and deep is the love of Christ, and to know this love that surpasses knowledge—that you may be filled to the measure of all the fullness of God.
>
> —Ephesians 3:16–19

I can remember that, in the depths of my concern, in the brokenness and loneliness in my life, I found that the Spirit of God strengthened me inside, where Christ abides. And I have found that He is everything He said He would be. When I cried out to him, the eternal One did exceeding abundantly beyond what I could even ask or think.

Your Life Choices Affect Eternity

Then Jesus said to his disciples, "If anyone would come after me, he must deny himself and take up his cross and follow me. For whoever wants to save his life will lose it, but whoever loses his life for me will find it. What good will it be for a man if he gains the whole world, yet forfeits his soul? Or what can a man give in exchange for his soul? For the Son of Man is going to come in his Father's glory with his angels, and then he will reward each person according to what he has done."

—Matthew 16:24–27

You may already be familiar with this passage, but how thoroughly have you applied it to eternal things? You may assume that these verses are about an eternal reward. But every choice you make affects eternity itself. Jesus suffered on the cross in obedience to the Father's great love for us. When you take up your cross, it is intended to be the same: out of God's great love for us, you would allow Him to sacrifice

He will turn the hearts of the fathers to their children, and the hearts of the children to their fathers.

—Malachi 4:6

you, too. By your obedience, even to losing your life, you and every sacrificial believer will find life itself by sharing God's eternal purpose. That is why Jesus calls His disciples to deny self and follow Him. Otherwise, all our choices are based on self-interests and not on what God intended by His example.

Serving Self vs. Serving Eternity

Jesus' attitude toward some unbelieving Samaritans dramatizes the difference between serving self and serving eternity. As He made His way back to Jerusalem, toward the end of His earthly ministry, He sent messengers on ahead to a Samaritan village to get things ready for Him to stay for the night. However, the villagers were not pleased that He was heading for Jerusalem and would not welcome Him.

Two of Jesus' disciples, James and John, believed the villagers had earned some consequences for their rudeness to Jesus. "'Lord, do you want us to call fire down from heaven to destroy them?' But Jesus turned and rebuked them and they went to another village" (Luke 9:54–56). James and John believed that God would provide them the power to destroy the offending Samaritans for rejecting the Messiah. Jesus' response was to rebuke the disciples and go to another village, where they were received. Burning up the Samaritans might have satisfied the disciples' desire for credibility but not God's eternal ways.

Some time later, after the persecution of the church in Jerusalem had scattered believers throughout the region, the people of Samaria had another opportunity to encounter the power of God. This time the followers of Christ brought life instead of the threat of destruction.

> Those who had been scattered preached the word wherever they went. Philip went down to a city in Samaria and proclaimed the Christ there. When the crowds heard Philip and saw the miraculous signs he did, they all paid close attention to what he said. With shrieks, evil spirits came out of many, and many paralytics and cripples were healed. So there was great joy in that city.
> —Acts 8:4–8

Which approach to the Samaritans best reflects God's desire for eternity—that of James and John or that of Jesus? James and John were justified in disapproving of the treatment Jesus received on His journey, but they were not justified in wanting to thwart God's purpose of redeeming the world, even those Samaritans and those who would deny hospitality to Christ. In God's provision the gospel came to flourish in this same region. Again, God's eternal ways provided for life. John had the blessing of seeing what God would do with those who had once rejected Him.

"When the apostles in Jerusalem heard that Samaria had accepted the word of God, they sent Peter and John to them. When they arrived, they prayed for them that they might receive the Holy Spirit" (Acts 8:14–15).

Eternal Consequences

Taking up the cross for God's eternal purpose means to love one another, even as Christ loved those who did and would reject Him. Another familiar passage that may not be plowed as deeply as it needs to be is Romans 10:11–12. "As the Scripture says, 'Anyone who trusts in him will never be put to shame.' For there is no difference between Jew and Gentile—the same Lord is Lord of all and richly blesses all who call on him, for 'Everyone who calls on the name of the Lord will be saved.'"

Failing to love a brother may turn him away from a closer walk with God at a time when God may want to call him to missions. Failing to love a brother, or to count anyone as unlovable, rebukes Christ for His sacrifice. Scripture says that everyone who calls on the name of the Lord will be saved (Rom. 10:9–10). Everyone who is saved is a new creation in Christ. Everyone who is saved is a child of God, an heir and a joint-heir with Christ (Rom. 8:16–17). This would be a good opportunity for fear and trembling for all of us as we reflect on those we have rejected, ignored, or avoided! For, in the cause of Christ, there is no self-selected service.

> Remember those earlier days after you had received the light, when you stood your ground in a great contest in the face of suffering. Sometimes you were publicly exposed to insult and persecution; at other times you stood side by side with those who were so treated. . . . You need to persevere so that when you have done the will of God, you will receive what he has promised. . . . We are not of those who shrink back and are destroyed, but of those who believe and are saved.
> —Hebrews 10:32–33, 36, 39

Eternal Impact

The eighth chapter of Acts complements the eternal impact of the Great Commission of Matthew 28 by describing how the gospel is spread. "How, then, can they call on the one they have not believed in? And how can they believe in the one of whom they have not heard? And how can they hear without someone preaching to them? And how can they preach unless they are sent? As it is written, 'How beautiful are the feet of those who bring good news!'" (Rom. 10:14–15).

The Word of God presents the way to eternal life. In addition to bringing eternal life to others, the spread of the gospel is also the key activity in affecting eternity. Any reluctance to participate limits those whom God desires to involve in bringing His eternal good news of eternal life.

Eternal Reconciliation

Christ came to reconcile us eternally to the Father. This is accomplished through Christ, even as believers in Him share the same Spirit of Christ that makes unity in the Spirit possible. The command of God to be reconciled to one another puts His people in a relationship with Him, so that He can touch lives for eternity. A church split is a refusal to obey Christ's command to reconcile. Unresolved adversity between members of a congregation also ignores their relationship as a body of believers. "If one part suffers, every part suffers with it; if one part is honored, every part rejoices with it" (1 Cor. 12:26).

As a result of a church split, eternity is always affected in a cumulative way. If one life feels a call to missions or ministry, that one life can begin to touch people, and many of those feel a touch from God and those they touch do also. If dissension among believers distracts or prevents lives from hearing the call of God, eternity is affected.

Serving Eternity

Many see their actions in an isolated way. In God's eternal ways, one person is not just one person. One person represents the many God desires to reach through the service of one yielded life. If a whole denomination loses sight of God's eternal purpose, the cumulative effect of their disobedience is staggering. Over time, what will be the eternal impact of their choices?

When believers think of serving God in terms of a career choice, a personality match, or as part of their search for personal fulfillment, disobedience seems permissible even though eternity is not served. That is when mans' ways take the place of God's ways. If we guide children toward being safe and successful in a profession instead of being yielded to God's eternal purpose, whatever and wherever that may lead, we oppose God's ways and replace them with our own. If we fail to see partial obedience to God as disobedience, we will be blind to what might have been, if we had been obedient to God.

The Ways of God

God's ways are not our ways, but He desires that we know them, so we can be shaped and changed by them (Ps. 119:117–120). The perfect example of God's way is His Son, our Savior, Jesus Christ. Do you not believe that the Scripture says that God's goal is to conform you to the image of His Son? Do you suppose that in addition to that He has also placed His Spirit within us so that His Son can live in us by His Spirit? Then allow Jesus Christ to live out His life through you. Paul says, "I have been crucified with Christ and I no longer live, but Christ lives in me. The life I live in the body, I live by faith in the Son of God, who loved me and gave himself for me" (Gal. 2:20).

The clearest way to know the ways of God is to know Him personally through His Son, His Spirit, and His Word. When we have Christ living within us, we can begin to understand God's ways of love, God's sovereign ways, His ways of holiness and truth, and His eternal ways. As God transforms us into His image, we can function in His ways and serve His purpose.

A prayer of the psalmist seems the most appropriate way to close this short attempt to sketch some of the ways of God and try to be of help in calling believers to follow them:

> You are my portion, O LORD;
> > I have promised to obey your words.
> I have sought your face with all my heart;
> > be gracious to me according to your promise.

I have considered my ways
    and have turned my steps to your statutes.
I will hasten and not delay
    to obey your commands.
Though the wicked bind me with ropes,
    I will not forget your law.
At midnight I rise to give you thanks
    for your righteous laws.
I am a friend to all who fear you,
    to all who follow your precepts.
The earth is filled with your love, O LORD;
    teach me your decrees.
                —Psalm 119:57–64

Think About—Pray About

Believers are surrounded by proof that God is always dealing with the eternity of those around us. God commands Christians to share His eternal ways and perspective so they can join Him in His work of bearing witness to the world (Matt. 28:19–20). "The end of all things is near. Therefore be clear minded and self-controlled so that you can pray. Above all, love each other deeply, because love covers over a multitude of sins" (1 Pet. 4:7–8).

- Those moments when our behavior reflects our belief in God's eternal truth are part of how we demonstrate our faithfulness at the most basic level. God's response is eternal in scope and entrusts us with greater opportunities to serve and witness to His eternal ways. Are you living faithfully?

- An eternal relationship with our eternal God is possible through the Lord Jesus Christ. How often do you confront others about the most important matter in all of time or eternity? How often do you confront yourself with a scriptural gauge, such as Ephesians 3:16, to take measure of the Spirit's presence and activity in your life? Think about it.

- Jesus told Peter that he held the keys to the kingdom (Matt 16:19). The keys are Truth, and what every disciple does with them affects eternity. To choose not to walk in God's ways equals eternal losses. Not to go at Christ's command equals leaving multitudes in eternal darkness and eternal hell. Pray about it.

Conducting a Group Study of *The Ways of God*

This Group Study Guide provides:
- Ideas for the Group Leader
- Easy-to-use Discussion Topics

Read the book content and the guide before planning a group study.

Group Leader Ideas

Who? A small group study of *The Ways of God* is appropriate for Bible study groups, accountability groups, discipleship and prayer groups, and for one-to-one discipling. These ideas are aimed toward adult believers.

When? Get together at a time that works for your group. Allow for at least thirty minutes of discussion and prayer. However, let the Holy Spirit determine your schedule. These suggestions are intended as a framework; be sensitive to the concerns and needs of the people in your group.

Where?   Plan to meet at a church, in a home or business, or for a meal at a local restaurant; anywhere conducive for discussion and prayer.

How?   Use the group suggestions in this section. Before each group session, as group leader you should:

• Pray for each group member.
• Study the chapter the group will discuss.
• Encourage the people in the group.
• Get in touch with anyone who missed the last session.

God bless you as you facilitate your small group.

GROUP DISCUSSION GUIDE

CHAPTER 1

God's Ways Are Not Our Ways

1. Based on the insights offered in chapter 1, ask a couple of people in the group to explain what is meant by the title of chapter 1, "God's Ways Are Not Our Ways."

Read Isaiah 55:6–11 aloud. Then invite the group to draw from it as they discuss its implications for them.

> Seek the LORD while he may be found;
>   call on him while he is near.
> Let the wicked forsake his way
>   and the evil man his thoughts.
> Let him turn to the LORD, and he will have mercy on him,
>   and to our God, for he will freely pardon.
>
> "For my thoughts are not your thoughts,
>   neither are my ways your ways,"
>   declares the LORD.

"As the heavens are higher than the earth,
     so are my ways higher than your ways
     and my thoughts than your thoughts.
As the rain and the snow
     come down from heaven,
and do not return to it
     without watering the earth
and making it bud and flourish,
     so that it yields seed for the sower and bread for the
          eater,
so is my word that goes out of my mouth."
                                        —Isaiah 55:6–11a

2. Let the group know that God's desire is that all believers
would grow to become more like Christ (2 Cor. 3:18). Doing
that requires knowing and practicing God's ways. Ask volun-
teers to discuss how they could have applied God's ways instead
of their own to one of the situations they have faced in the past
week (i.e. not blowing up; willing to serve others; seeing others
as cherished ones God loves and sacrificed His Son to save).

3. Ask the group to help you compile a list of the ways of
God based on chapter 1. How do these translate into godly
character in their lives? Discuss.

4. Read this quote from "Think About—Pray About," in
chapter 1. "When God gives you insight into the weaknesses
of others, the insight is given for intercession, not criticism."
How does this represent a way of God? Discuss.

5. Dismiss with sentence prayers asking God for more of His
ways to become apparent in the lives of group members.

CHAPTER 2

The Ways of God Are Love

1. Before the group gathers, think about how much God loves each one in the group. Ask yourself how you have allowed God to demonstrate His love for them through your words and actions. Pray for each member of the group, asking God to give you His love and compassion for them all.

2. Remind the group that they must have all experienced how easy it is to love some people and how hard it seems even to tolerate others. Ask, "What kinds of distinctions does God make when it comes to loving people?" Read this Scripture to the group: "For God so loved the world that he gave his one and only Son, that whoever believes in him shall not perish but have eternal life" (John 3:16). Ask, "According to this verse, whom does God love?" Discuss how this certainty of God's love for everyone affects us as individual believers.

3. Say, "God's way of love gives without any assurance of being loved back. God even loves the ungodly." Read aloud the following verses to the group. "You see, at just the right time, when we were still powerless, Christ died for the ungodly. Very rarely will anyone die for a righteous man, though for a good man someone might possibly dare to die. But God demonstrates his own love for us in this: While we were still sinners, Christ died for us" (Rom. 5:6–8). Ask the group to discuss how they could acquire the same sacrificial, unconditional love that God has shown us. Tell them this love is a result of God's presence. Ask how they could encourage one another to show the love of God they have received.

4. In love, God commands us to obey Him, because the Father's commands bring life. How are God's commands gifts to us? Based on chapter 1, how does obedience help us to experience the love of God?

5. Invite the group to pray silently for at least a minute, asking God to show them how to live His way of love. Close with a prayer of commitment to trust and obey God's way of love.

CHAPTER 3

The Ways of God Are Sovereign

1. Imagine that you have been summoned by a king and given the full responsibility for a whole regiment of soldiers. A sovereign can do that. How would you communicate clearly the wishes of the sovereign?

Now examine the impact it can make when God calls a believer to serve Him by guiding people through God's care and influence. Do you know what Sovereign God requires of a believer who understands that God calls all believers to His service? All believers have the responsibility of following God's orders and guiding those He places around them. Review chapter 3 and share these summary thoughts with the group.

2. Read Isaiah 50:10–11:

"Who among you fears the LORD
    and obeys the word of his servant?

> Let him who walks in the dark,
>   who has no light,
> trust in the name of the LORD
>   and rely on his God.
> But now, all you who light fires
>   and provide yourselves with flaming torches,
> go, walk in the light of your fires
>   and of the torches you have set ablaze.
> This is what you shall receive from my hand;
>   you will lie down in torment."
>
> —Isaiah 50:10–11

Ask the group to discuss the difference between trusting God for light when you are in the dark and trusting yourself when you are in the dark and making your own light.

3. Say to the group, "If God is ruler over everything, how much should we worry about life? If we are obeying God's Word because God is Sovereign, what does that leave us to worry about? Does that mean nothing will ever seem difficult or even scary? Consider Daniel; wise or foolhardy?" Discuss.

4. How does knowing that God is Sovereign affect what and how we give to God? Ask someone to explain what bearing the fact that everything belongs to God could have on how much of God's property we give back to Him.

5. Invite the group to pray for one another, thanking God for giving each one to the group.

GROUP DISCUSSION GUIDE

CHAPTER 4

The Ways of God Are Holy

1. In a time of prayer before your group meets, read 1 Peter 2:9–10, and meditate on all the implications it has for you. "You are a chosen people, a royal priesthood, a holy nation, a people belonging to God, that you may declare the praises of him who called you out of darkness into his wonderful light. Once you were not a people, but now you are the people of God." Prepare to read this to the group and ask the group, What does it mean to be the people of God? How do the people of God show God's holiness?

2. In chapter 4, it says, "When God has a people rightly related to Him, He is able to display His glory to a watching world." Ask the group to discuss examples of how they have seen God display His glory to a watching world.

3. Is it easier to trust someone you know than someone you do not know? What about when a complete stranger offers life-saving assistance in an emergency? In both cases, the friend or stranger is set apart to help you. Point out to the group that such circumstances and matters of trust narrow our focus. How does living set apart for God's use narrow and direct our focus as believers? Discuss.

4. Ask, "How is sin the opposite of holiness?" Say, "The difference between sin and holiness is that sin is rebellion against God and holiness is being totally set apart for God's purpose and service. Although everyone sins, believers have Christ living out His life in them." Ask the group to consider and pray about this becoming the reality of life for them as believers.

5. Request that a volunteer voice a prayer for greater holiness for each one in the group, calling each by name in the prayer. Close the prayer time by asking each one to partner with another group member and pray in the coming week for each other's yieldedness to God's way of holiness.

CHAPTER 5

The Ways of God Are True

1. Before the group session, enlist one or two members of the group to be prepared to share examples of how God has shown them that He is the Truth. Ask them to provide Scripture that reflects their examples.

2. During the session, call on the ones enlisted to share their examples and Scrsiptures. When they have finished, say to the group, Freedom comes from knowing that God is Truth, that He is reliable and trustworthy, and He will do everything that He has said He will do, in His timing and in His way. Ask the group to discuss how trusting God brings freedom, and how knowing that God is true differs from trusting in God.

3. Ask the group if any of them has ever had an opportunity to take an important message to someone. Ask a volunteer to

share his example. Read the following: "We are therefore Christ's ambassadors, as though God were making his appeal through us. We implore you on Christ's behalf: Be reconciled to God" (2 Cor. 5:20). Ask the group, "If you had information that would save millions, wouldn't you try to deliver that message? God has already put His Holy Spirit in the world to draw people to Him, but what if you could be used by God to confirm that truth for some and see them trust God?" Discuss.

4. God functions in Truth. That truth includes the fact that He loves us and deals with us in perfect, consistent love. If God lives in you, how should you function? How can His truth be seen in you at home? At church? At work?

5. Invite the group to request prayer for themselves to function in Truth. List the requests and ask for individuals to volunteer to pray for each request as you read them aloud, separately, between prayers.

CHAPTER 6

The Ways of God Are Eternal

1. Begin by reminding the group of the opening Scripture from the start of the study, Isaiah 55:8–9.

> "For my thoughts are not your thoughts,
>   neither are your ways my ways,"
>   declares the Lord.
> "As the heavens are higher than the earth,
>   so are my ways higher than your ways
>   and my thoughts than your thoughts."

Ask, "How concerned is God about eternity in His thoughts and ways?"

2. Ask the group to discuss how their behavior reflects their belief in God's eternal Truth. Ask them how their behavior based on Truth demonstrates their faithfulness to God, Who is Truth. Discuss, waiting if necessary, for participants to

gather their thoughts. Ask the group how their faithfulness to God touches eternity.

3. Read aloud to the group, Ephesians 3:16: "I pray that out of his glorious riches he may strengthen you with power through his Spirit in your inner being . . ." Say, God's power is eternal. His presence in your life is the presence of the Eternal. When you are strengthened by Gods power through His Spirit, how close is God's power to anyone who is near you? How close is God's power to anyone you witness to? Discuss.

4. In Matthew 16, Jesus told Peter that he held the keys to the kingdom. The keys are Truth, and what every disciple does with them affects eternity. To choose not to walk in God's ways equals eternal losses. To not go at Christ's command equals leaving multitudes in eternal darkness and eternal hell. Ask the group to discuss what God could do through them and how it could affect eternity.

5. Pray specifically about how God will make use of the group's awareness of His ways. Pray that He will bless through them. Ask them to bow their heads while you read Hebrews 11:32–38 from your Bible. Ask them to meditate on this passage and silently pray that they will live obediently to whatever God requires of them.

Say, We know that God's ways differ from the world's ways. Man is always aware of time and his desires. God is not bound by time, and His greatest desire is to draw all people to Himself. When God involves us in His purposes, He may reveal Himself to others by our witness, both through the abundance that comes from Him and by the sufferings He strengthens us to bear. In every situation, our response to God is a witness to the world that God loves them. By our love and trust, regardless of circumstance, we show that God is worthy of their love and trust.

About the Authors

Henry T. Blackaby has spent his life in ministry. Beginning in 1958, he served churches in California and Canada as music director, Christian education director, and senior pastor.

Dr. Blackaby served on staff at the North American Mission Board of the Southern Baptist Convention in Alpharetta, Georgia, as Special Assistant to the President. Through the Office of Revival and Spiritual Awakening, he provided leadership to thousands of pastors and laypersons across North America. He also served as Special Assistant to the Presidents of the International Mission Board and LifeWay Christian Resources.

In the early 1990s Henry Blackaby became one of North America's best-selling Christian authors, committing the rest of his life to helping people know and experience God. Among Dr. Blackaby's books are *Experiencing God, Fresh Encounter, Experiencing God Day-by-Day, The Experience: Day by Day with God,* and *The Man God Uses.*

Henry Blackaby and his wife Marilynn have five married children: Richard, Thomas, Melvin, Norman, and Carrie. All are working in Christian ministry. He currently serves as president of Henry Blackaby Ministries.

Roy T. Edgemon was born in Texas, though his family moved to Tennessee soon after, returning when he was eleven. He met his wife-to-be, Anna Marie, in college. The two have been ministering together ever since in pastorates, international missions, and North American missions. For twenty-three years Roy led an area of Southern Baptist Convention denominational work that came to be known as the Discipleship and Family Group of LifeWay Church Resources. He has been directly responsible for publishing a number of successful discipleship resources and has authored many books, including *The Doctrines Baptists Believe*, *Foundations of Our Faith*, and *Jesus by Heart*. Roy and his wife, Anna Marie, have one daughter, Lori Shepard. She and husband, Douglas, parent the Edgemon's precocious grandchildren, Nathan Roy and Sarah Elizabeth.